WAGiLabs
PlayBook

**An Idea Incubator for Kids' Ideas
that will Change the World!**

AUTHORS

Chic Thompson

Chic's passion is inspiring executives, MBA students and children to be "curious first... critical second" while creative problem solving. He is a Fellow at the University Virginia's Darden Business School and adjunct faculty at the Brookings Institution.

In 2001, Harvard Business School released a case study on the speaking career of Chic entitled "What a Great Idea!."

Chic's first book, "What a Great Idea!," published by HarperCollins, was a main selection of the Executive Book Club. His second book, "Yes, But..." is a guide to overcoming the bureaucratic language that stifles continuous innovation. He wrote this book after consulting with GE to help design their continuous improvement process called "Work-Out."

Chic worked in new product development and marketing for:
- W.L. Gore and Associates (Gore-Tex®)
- Johnson & Johnson
- Walt Disney

During the last 30 years, Chic has given over 4500 presentations and has teamed up with talent ranging from Tony Robbins and Stephen Covey to Cirque du Soleil and Second City Improv.

Sandy Damashek

A pioneer in children's interactive media, Sandy helped launch the Interactive Group at Sesame Workshop. Since then, she has been at the forefront of digital media - producing and writing the preschool channel of AT&T's iTV trial, producing interactive movies for The Amazing Space children's museum and collaborating on the Word World prototype for Play TV's mobile platform, and, most recently, serving as Creative Producer, Interactive for 8 math-based Umig.

Sandy has also written more than 30 non-fiction and fiction children's books.

(Curiosity + Connection + Courage) = Social Innovation

kids

An INNOVATION is a new idea that helps overcome a challenge. Social innovation helps overcome a challenge that affects people, e.g., by reducing costs, helping people in need, or improving community life.

Put simply: social innovation is making a change in the world for good. **It's doing better, together.**

A social KIDpreneur is any kid who uses curiosity, connection, and courage to come up with great ideas to solve challenges in his or her community or in the world.

WHAT WE BELIEVE:

To some adults, the idea that kids can think like scientists and design like entrepreneurs seems absurd. They feel that kids are impulsive, unpredictable, and live only for the moment. As experienced educators and entrepreneurs we believe differently.

We **BELIEVE** that when you are a kid you naturally have curiosity, empathy, and endless ideas. When cultivated instead of squelched, these skills will help you grow and become an adult with a mindset of possibilities and collaboration.

We **BELIEVE** that inventing is contagious and the bug to become a future social entrepreneur is *"caught not taught"* when kids are young, especially at the ages of 8-11.

We **BELIEVE** today's globalization means more competition. What's more, a competitive culture means that we need more ideas, better ideas, and the skill to collaborate on ideas.

We **BELIEVE** that the jobs that are disappearing today will be re-created or reinvented possibly by kids tomorrow.

We **BELIEVE** in leaving WAGi footprints that will become a pathway to invention for kids around the world to follow.

WHAT IS WAGiLabs ALL ABOUT?

WAGiLabs is all about play. And ideas. And most importantly... **Doing good to help people.**

When kids play together, their imaginations come together, and new ideas happen! In the WAGiLabs, kids connect with kids (in their community and in distant places) to learn from each other, share ideas, innovate, and make people's lives better. Through curiosity, connection, and courage, kids can change the world!

Learning Objectives:

Curiosity:
- Discovering your passions (what you love)
- "Walking in the shoes of others" (practicing empathy)
- Being a detective (exploring your neighborhood, community, the world)
- Uncovering needs and problems

Connection:
- Teaming up with other kids
- Comparing and choosing team goals (needs and problems to solve)
- Brainstorming solutions
- Striving for innovation (thinking out of the box)
- Sharing ideas with those in need and those who can help
- Responding to feedback, revising ideas
- Building prototypes: cooperating, assigning & sharing roles

Courage:
- Planning a presentation to pitch ideas
- Pitching ideas at **Guppy Tank**.
- Turning ideas into actions that will do good
- Learning through trial and error
- Not giving up when there are problems or obstacles
- Selling ideas to get support from others and investment
- Establishing a network of kidpreneurs
- Playing it forward

Kids:
- Target age: 8-11 years' old
- Location: anywhere kids want to dream big, do good, get messy, and change the world!

WHAT IS A WAGiLabs MISSION?

A Mission is one day's session focused on an aspect of entrepreneurship that includes any or all of the following:

 WAGi Cheer (5 minutes) - To start each mission, kids say the WAGi Cheer:

Wonder
(Arms out, palms up)

Yes, **A**ND
(Hi-five)

Get Messy
(Both arms circle up & out in front of body)

I Can
(Fist pump)

 Welcome (5 minutes) - An intro to the Mission's goals and focus.

 Flashback Chat (5 minutes) - Review of previous session and reinforce the activities and the learnings.

 Explore: Get Messy! (60 minutes) - Teambuilding and creative activities that explore the process of being an inventor and KIDpreneur.

 Brain Breaks! (5 minutes) - A chance for kids to get up and move with music and activities.

 Wrap Up (5 minutes) - Discussion where kids share thoughts and conclusions about the day's Mission.

 Log In: Write & Reflect (5 minutes) - Quiet time for kids to think about their experiences and write notes and draw pictures in their Log Book.

NOTE:
The WAGi Playbook includes prompts to help you introduce the concepts and activities in each Mission. Feel free to use or adapt these prompts in any way that works for you and your group. The time suggested for each activity is also flexible. You can extend activity time if needed, as long as individual reflection is included at the end of each day. If necessary, a Wrap Up discussion can be included at the beginning of the next WAGI mission (during the Flashback chat).

WHO IS WAGI?

Wagi, our tireless mascot, inspires us to follow the "Wagi Ways" every day. He captains each mission, and reminds us to dream big, do good, share ideas, and keep going until we reach our goals.

Wagi comes from a long line of creative canines with a mission to do good things. His ancestor, Barko Polo, was Marco Polo's constant companion, sniffing out the safest path along the Silk Road. A distant cousin, Flea-onardo had long, flapping ears that inspired Leonardo da Vinci's very first sketch of a helicopter. And let's not forget the feline-chasing, tree shaking I-Sic Newton. When she chased the neighbor's cat up a tree, an apple tumbled to the ground, and her pal Isaac Newton discovered gravity!

Invention has been the goal of Wagi's life as well. His cartoonist neighbor, Rube Goldberg invented the Mouse Trap Game. And sharing Wagi's do good tendencies, Rube invented the dog-assisted safety device for walking on icy pavements.

© 2016 Rube Goldberg. All rights reserved.

Wagi's ancestors and Rube inspire him to think about ways that he can help others and be a best friend, too. He strives for innovation and stretches the bounds of conventions. In fact, his latest idea is an umbrella for both an owner and a dog. Below is a drawing of his prototype.

To inspire others, Wagi has launched WAGiLabs, an innovation incubator where kids can share ideas and collaborate to make the world a better place. He invites kids to join the journey to become KIDpreneurs, and can't wait to see the drawings and prototypes they create!

WELCOME ABOARD
THE HMS ENTREPRENEUR**SHIP**?

Discover more about yourself, the world, and the power of ideas to **IMPROVE LIVES**!

WHERE ARE WE GOING?

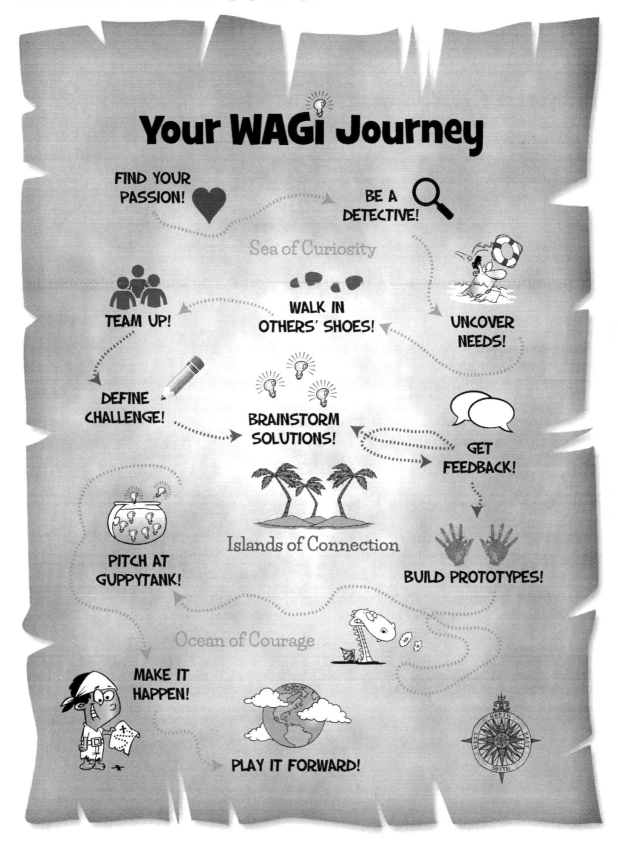

WAGiLabs MISSIONS:

CURIOSITY

1. Find Your Passion!
Which passions do you share with others? Which are yours only? In the WAGiLab, your passions can help you come up with ideas. Let's discover the things we love and love to do.

2. Be a Detective!
The WAGiLab is all about coming up with ideas to make life better. Before we can help people, let's do some investigation to see what people need.

3. Uncover Needs!
What makes people unhappy? You guessed it! When they don't have the things they need, or when there are dangers in their community or when they don't feel safe. Time for more detective work!

4. Walk in Others' Shoes!
By trying on other people's shoes and walking in them, we can see life as they see it, and feel what they feel. That is called having empathy. Having empathy is how we understand the changes that are needed in the world. Let's try on shoes to see through others' eyes.

CONNECTION

5. Team Up!
It's time to team up, talk together, and decide which needs we want to work on. Wagi Mate teams evaluate our list of neighborhood needs, and pick one need to tackle.

6. Define Challenge!
Defining a challenge means thinking about problems and goals. How can we look at our need as a challenge that we want to solve? Let's find out!

7. Brainstorm Day #1: Seeking Solutions!
Get ready to put on your thinking cap. On our first Brainstorming Day, everyone gets to share lots and lots of ideas - and no one says "NO!"

Brainstorm Day #2: Getting Wild and Crazy!
On our second Brainstorming Day, we stretch our minds to see what's good about our ideas, and come up with our wildest ideas yet!

8. **Get Feedback!**
   Feedback from others helps us improve our ideas and build the confidence to make them real. Let's reach out to others to learn what they think!

9. **Build Prototypes! Day #1:**
   Now that we have ideas, it is time to experiment with possible solutions. Let's build models or prototypes of possible solutions, and share them with others to see how they work.

   Build Prototypes! Day #2:
   Do our prototypes work? Are there problems? Do we have to make changes? Through the ups and downs of the inventing process, we learn that persistence and resilience are keys to turning our ideas into action. Don't give up!

COURAGE

10. **Plan Your Pitch!**
    What's the best way to present your ideas to your class, parents, teachers, members of the community? A perfect pitch, of course. Let's learn how to tell a story that makes our ideas irresistible!

11. **GuppyTank Practice! Day #1**
    Practice... practice... practice.

    GuppyTank Practice! Day #2
    And more practice.

12. **Go Go GuppyTank!**
    It's Show Time – time to celebrate and share the hard work of our WAGiLab teams. Kids have used detective skills to uncover needs in our community. They used brainstorming skills to come up with ideas to help solve those needs. Now it's time to present our ideas and solutions to our panel of coaches who will help turn these ideas into reality.

13. **Make It Happen!**
    Great ideas are only great when we make them happen. Let's look at the steps we need to take to make our ideas real, and take a big step forward by writing to mentors. We're on our way!

14. **Play It Forward!**
    In our last session, our WAGiLab teammates reflect on their experiences, and become coaches to help other kids learn the WAGi Way.

Sixteen 90-minute Sessions = **24 Hours to Change the World!**

Which passions do you share with others? Which are yours only? In the WAGiLab, your passions can help you come up with ideas.

Let's discover the things we love and love to do.

WAGiLabs MISSION 1:
Find Your Passion! *(90 minutes)*

WAGi Welcome *(5 minutes)*

Goal: Introduce WAGiLabs

Skills: Curiosity, Connection

[Begin by introducing yourself.]

GUIDE:

Welcome to the WAGiLab! WAGi (W-A-G-I) stands for "What A Great Idea!" I know ALL of you have great ideas, and I can't wait to hear them!

In the WAGiLab we're going to play with each other AND with our ideas to make them even more amazing. Not just for us, but for other people, too. Because the WAGiLab is all about using our ideas to help make the world a better place!

The Name Game *(20 minutes)*

Goal: Kids share names and learn about each other

Skills: Curiosity, Connecting, Listening, Yes and…

Needs: Name Tag Stickers, Colored Markers, Crayons, or Pencils

Prep: Make name tag for each Guide.

[Gather in a group. Have everyone make a nametag and put it on. When you see that kids have finished their tags, ring the WAGiLab bell so kids know it's time to wrap up. Use this bell to signal the end of each lab activity.]

GUIDE:

Look around. We're all very different. That's one reason we're going to be a fantastic team - because we each see things in our own special way. Have you ever been on a team before?

[Kids suggest sports teams, teams at school, fundraising teams, and others.]

GUIDE:

What makes a good team?

[Ideas might include working together, listening, having people with different skills or talents, splitting up work, planning, not leaving anyone out, etc. Respond to the first idea AND all ideas by saying… Yes, AND… Explain that in the WAGiLab, it's important to say Yes, AND to ALL ideas.]

GUIDE:

"Yes, AND…" is our first WAGi Way - or rule to live by. When someone shares an idea, we always say: "Yes, AND…" That means "I accept your idea… AND I'm ready for more!"

[As kids share their thoughts, encourage teammates to say "YES, and…" after each idea. Expand the list if kids need help. Then move to introductions.]

GUIDE:

Great ideas. WAGi Mates. Now, if we're going to work as a team, we'd better get to know each other better!

[Pair kids up and let them introduce themselves to each other by saying their names. After they do, continue.]

GUIDE:

Now that you know each other's names, do you feel like you really know each other? Probably not! Most of us just met. So let's take things a step further. I'll go first…

[Introduce yourself and share two personal bits of info that help the kids get to know more about you - what you like to do, what you don't like, your favorite food, hobby, or type of music, the name of your pet, where you'd like to take a trip, how many brothers and sisters you have - you get the idea!]

GUIDE:

What new things did you learn about me?

[Let kids answer.]

Good listening! That's another important WAGi Way! When you listen, someone else's idea might make you think of a new one, or you might find out that you like the same things!

Okay, WAGi Mates, help your partner get to know you. Tell about one or two things that make you... you! Partners, listen carefully because it will be up to you to introduce your new pal to the rest of our WAGi team.

[Give kids a few minutes to share. Remind them to listen closely so they will be able to introduce and tell about their partner. Walk around and help kids who are feeling shy or having trouble sharing. Suggest telling about favorite foods, hobbies, pets, or other things that are not too personal. After a few minutes, ring the WAGi bell. Then go around the circle, and let kids introduce their new Wagi Pals. Celebrate each introduction by having the whole team greet each person together.]

Brain Break! *(5 minutes)*

Goal: Give kids a chance to be active and take a break from quiet activities.

Skills: Be active, move

Needs: Music CDs and music player or streamed WAGiLab Playlist on our website

[After kids have been sitting and sharing, they might be a little antsy. If you think they need a little "physical" time, spend 5 minutes doing this Move It! activity. If movement will be disruptive or kids are still focused, feel free to skip this activity.]

Are you feeling antsy? I am! C'mon, let's take a little break... Get up, get out, and MOVE IT!

[Turn on Music, jump up and move around - dancing or just shaking your body. Encourage kids to do the same by moving in any way they like.]

Passion Makes Perfect! *(45 minutes)*

Goals: Kids talk about their passions, and learn which ones they share with others

Skills: Listening, Curiosity, Sharing, Connection

Needs: Pads of Sticky Notes, Markers and Writing Tools, Large board to display notes

[Sit in a circle on the ground or in chairs.]

GUIDE:

The introductions you did were great! Now we're going to learn even more about each other by creating a list of our passions. I'll show you what I mean.

[Hold up the Wagi "Passions" Poster and act as Wagi]

What is Wagi passionate about?

GUIDE:

Pretend I'm Wagi. Here's how I'd think about my passions...

"Hmmm... what do I like to do more than anything else? I know! I like being a detective searching for clues. And I really love chasing Fuzzy, the cat who lives next door. And I guess one of my passions is Frisbee - because I play every day!!"

Check out Wagi's passions on this poster. Now think about your passions. Would any of you choose Frisbee, like Wagi? Or do you like another sport better? What do you like to do more than anything else?

[Get suggestions from the kids. Identify each activity or idea as a passion. Follow each with: "Yes, AND..." does anyone else have a passion to share? After kids have come up with a few ideas, continue.]

GUIDE:

Now you're getting it! Let's play a game to find out more about your passions!

[Divide the group into 3 teams. Give each team a sheet of poster board. Then, pass around the sticky pads and ask everyone to take 3 sheets.

GUIDE:

To start, each of you write down three things you're passionate about. Use a separate sticky note for each one. When your team is ready, organize your sticky notes on the big sheet. Group passions that are alike.

16

[Walk around the room. If kids need help, suggest that passions can be things they like or do alone or with others, at home, at school, outside, or almost anyplace. Remind them of the things they talked about when they introduced themselves. Were any of them passions? Give kids 5 minutes to write down their ideas. Then remind them to start organizing their sticky notes. After 5 more minutes, ring the WAGiLab bell.]

Those passion boards are looking good! Now let's share and compare our teams' passions.

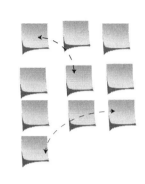

[Have a team leader from each team bring the team's big sheet up to the front. Then have all kids gather around the three team sheets. Together, let them continue organizing the sticky notes, with the team leaders moving notes between sheets to group similar passions together. Offer help if needed. Encourage kids to work out any disagreements among themselves. Again, give kids 10 minutes for this discussion.]

Wow! You have a lot of passions! But which ones are our WAGiLab favorites? It's time for your final votes!

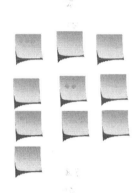

[Call kids up by team. Have each team member put 3 dots on his/her favorite passion, two blue dots on the second favorite, and one blue dot on the third favorite. When all WAGi kids have voted, count the dots and make a "TOP TEN LIST" of kid passions, and let kids read them out loud.]

We all see things in our own special way. Many of us share passions. Some of us have very unique passions. In the WAGiLab, our passions can help us come up with ideas, work together, and also choose the jobs that we do best. We're going to be a great team!

Wrap Up! *(5 minutes)*

Goals: Kids share thoughts about what they've explored in the day's mission

Skills: Listening, Curiosity, Sharing, Connection

Needs: Kids' Passions List, Log Books

[Sit in a circle or close together with the Kids' Passions List in view. Ask kids how they feel about their first day in the WAGiLab. If some kids are shy, it's okay if they just listen!]

GUIDE:

I can't believe it that our first WAGiLab's Mission is almost over! How do you feel about it? What did you learn about yourself and our team?

Let's take turns. And remember: When someone finished sharing, support their ideas by saying:" Yes, AND..."

[Let kids guide the conversation. After each team member finishes, say "Yes, AND..." Encourage others to say it with you. When everyone who wants to speak has had a chance, hand out the WAGi Log Books.]

Log In! *(5 minutes)*

Goals: Kids reflect further, and write or draw pictures in their personal logs to save their feelings, thoughts, and ideas about the Mission.

Skills: Reflection, Communicating ideas and feelings

Needs: Kids' Passions List, Log Books

[After logbooks have been handed out to team members.]

GUIDE:

These are your own, private logbooks for keeping a record of the things we do in the WAGiLab. First thing to do – write your name on the cover!

You can write ideas, draw pictures, tell about your feelings. It's all up to you. Take about 5 minutes to add thoughts or drawings about today's mission to your book!

[After kids have finished writing in their logbooks, collect the books.]

WAGi Cheer! *(5 minutes)*

Goals: Kids learn the WAGi Cheer they will say at the start and end of every day.

Skills: Listening, Sharing, Connection

Needs: WAGi Cheer Poster

*[Display the **WAGi Cheer poster**.]*

GUIDE:

Woohoo, what a day! But we can't let it end without learning the WAGi Cheer. It's our team promise that we'll share our ideas, play and work together, and follow our passions to make our ideas happen! So follow me!

[Chant the cheer as you act out each step.]

Wonder

(Arms out, palms up)

 # Yes, AND

(Hi-five)

Get Messy

(Both arms circle up & out in front of body)

 # I Can

(Fist pump)

WAGi!!!!!!

[Repeat and practice the cheer and actions until kids start to get it. End the day with a big cheer, and a reminder about the next WAGiLab meeting!]

Wonder

Yes, AND

Get Messy

I can

WAGi!!!

www.wagilabs.org

What is Wagi passionate about?

Be a Detective

The WAGiLab is all about coming up with ideas to make life better. Before we can help people, let's do some investigation to see what people need.

WAGILabs MISSION 2:

Be a Detective! *(90 minutes)*

Welcome: WAGi Cheer! *(5 minutes)*

Goals: Kids reconnect and build sense of team by chanting the WAGi Cheer

Skills: Connection, Teamwork

Needs: WAGi Cheer Poster, Nametags, Colored Markers, Crayons, or Pencils

[As kids arrive, have them make new nametags. When everyone's ready, stand in a circle. Display the WAGi Cheer poster.]

GUIDE:

Welcome back, lab-sters! Do you remember the WAGi Cheer we learned last time?

It's the perfect way to start our lab day and remind us of the 4 WAGi Ways: **Wonder** (or be curious) **Yes, AND** (play as a team) **Get Messy** (share lots of ideas), and **I Can** (use your passion to make ideas happen!)

Wonder
Yes, AND
Get Messy
I can
WAGi!!!

[Lead the cheer or let a volunteer to it. Chant as a team, and act out each step with lots of energy! For Yes, AND, don't forget to give each other a high five!]

GUIDE:

Wonder *(Arms out, palms up)*

Yes, AND *(Hi-five)*

Get Messy *(Both arms circle up & out in front of body)*

I Can *(Fist pump)*

WAGi!!!!!!

Flashback *(5 minutes)*

Goal: Reconnect kids with ideas and accomplishments from last lab experience

Skills: Curiosity, Connection, Compassion

Needs: Kids' Top 10 Passions List

Last session was smooth sailing! We began our journey by discovering our passions. Remind us of your favorites. Do you remember which passions made it to our Top Ten List?

[Before showing the list, see if kids can come up with any or all of the Top Ten passions. Show the list and let kids read the passions out loud.]

How Do They Do It? *(10 minutes)*

Goal: Introduce "detective" skills: observing, focusing on detail, asking questions, taking careful notes, using intuition, making logical connections

Skills: Curiosity, Connection, Detective Skills

Needs: Detective Questions, Detective Skills Poster, markers

GUIDE:

Today, we're going to do more detective work. But instead looking at ourselves, we're going to discover more about our neighborhood. When detectives want to learn more about a place, they use special skills.

[Hold up Detective Skills Poster.]

GUIDE:

Take a look! Wagi has many skills. Some are very important for for doing detective work. Others, not so much!

[Choose kids to come up and each circle one important detective skill (until all 6 detective skills have been identified: Asking Questions, Observing, Doing Research, Taking Notes, Making Connections, Uncovering Clues. Ask kids to give examples or explain when they might use each skill. Offer suggestions if kids have trouble. When kids have identified the 6 important skills, congratulate the team!]

Map It! *(30 minutes)*

Goal: Mapping, observing, focusing on detailsical connections

Skills: Curiosity, Connection, Detective Skills

Needs: Map Poster, Poster board or drawing paper, markers or crayons

Okay, detectives, the WAGiLab is all about ideas that make life better. The best place to start investigating what people need is our own neighborhood or community, so we can help people we know.

[Show the Wagi Neighborhood Map as a model. If possible, take the kids on a walk through the neighborhood before they make their maps. Otherwise, have kids imagine their neighborhood.]

Your observing skills can help you think about your neighborhood. Imagine your house. Now think of the places that are nearby. Make a map that shows your house and the places you can walk to, ride or drive to, or visit.

[Then tell kids they'll have 15 minutes to make their map. Kids can write word labels or draw simple pictures or icons to identify places. Suggest that kids who live in the same neighborhood can work together. After 10 minutes, signal that kids have 5 minutes left. When time's up, let kids share their maps with the whole group]

Brain Break! (Mirror, Mirror) *(5 minutes)*

[Guide jumps up, shakes, moves arms, etc.]

GUIDE:

My brain needs a break, and you know what that means. It's time for a challenge! Let's play Mirror, Mirror? Pair up! Choose one person to be the MoveMaster and one to be the Mirror!

[Explain that the Mirror has to follow every action the MoveMaster makes. Tell the MoveMasters to start moving slowly. Can the Mirrors match their moves? Switch roles, and let the Mirrors be MoveMasters. Switch back and forth a few times with each "challenge" lasting about 30 seconds. Start with small movements and as kids get the idea, have the Masters make bigger moves.]

Detective Training! *(30 minutes)*

Goal: Practice "detective" skills: observing, focusing on detail, asking questions, taking careful notes, using intuition, making logical connections

Skills: Curiosity, Connection, Detective Skills

Needs: Detective Questions, LogBooks

GUIDE:

Now, we can use the maps you made to do more detective work in your neighborhoods. And you can practice two more detective skills: asking questions and taking notes!

[Have kids choose partners to create teams of four. Teams who have worked on the same map can stay together for this follow-up activity. After kids partner up, hand out the Detective Questions List.]

GUIDE:

Here's a list of detective questions to help you learn more about your neighborhoods! As you ask each question, look at your map. Do any of the places help you think of answers? Do they have the best things in the neighborhood? Are they places where life is hard? Or places that you would like to change? If so, write the answers on the map. You can also add new places if you think of them.

[Before kids start, reassure them that it's okay if they feel shy or don't know the answer to any question. If one question doesn't work, just move on to another! Explain that respecting feelings and knowing the right questions to ask is a very special detective skill! Remind them to take good notes – on their maps or separate pieces of paper.]

GUIDE:

Take notes on your map or on paper about the good things and the problems you discover about your neighborhood.

[Give kids enough time to ask each other questions, listen to, and write down the answers. Then share the lists. Make a new combined list that separates the good things from the problems.]

Wrap Up! *(5 minutes)*

Goals: Kids share thoughts about what they've explored and learned in the mission

Skills: Listening, Curiosity, Sharing, Connection

Needs: Detective Skills Poster, Detective Questions, Log Books

[Sit in a circle or close together with the Detective Skills on display. Ask kids what they learned about being a detective. Was it easy to talk to their partners?]

GUIDE:

Let's talk about the detective work we did today. Did the questions you asked help you know more about your neighborhood or community? Did you discover anything that surprised you? Did some of you feel shy about answering questions? The more detective work you do, the better you'll be at asking the right questions and making people feel comfortable.

[Suggest that kids continue their detective work at home to see what they can discover by asking their brothers, sisters, other family members, and friends the same questions they asked each other! Remind them to be respectful if people don't want to answer! Hand out the WAGi LogBooks.]

Log In! *(5 minutes)*

Goals: Kids reflect further, and write or draw pictures in their personal logs to save their feelings, thoughts, and ideas about the Be a Detective Mission.

Skills: Reflection, Communicating ideas and feelings

Needs: Detective Questions, Log Books

[After LogBooks have been handed out to team members.]

GUIDE:

Add some thoughts or pictures to tell or show what you learned about your neighborhood and being a detective. Don't forget to tell how this day made you feel.

[After kids have finished writing in their LogBooks, collect the books.]

WAGi High Five! *(1 minutes)*

Wow, we sure did a lot of detective work today! Let's bring it all together with a WAGi High Five. All together now!

[End with a reminder about the next WAGiLab meeting!]

28

Detective Skills

Asking Questions

Uncovering Hidden Clues

Observing Details

Taking Notes

Doing Research

Connecting the Dots

Wagi's Neighborhood

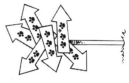

Factories

Park and Playground

SUPER MARKET

Shopping Area

Garden

Reduced Speed Zone

City Dump

Medical Services

School

Hang Out

www.wagilabs.org

Detective ???

1. What is life like in our neighborhood?

2. What is the best thing?

3. What is the hardest thing?

4. What would make life better for our neighborhood?

5. What would you change?

What makes people unhappy? You guessed it! When they don't have the things they need, or when there are dangers in their community or when they don't feel safe.

Time for more detective work!

WAGILabs MISSION 3:

Uncover Needs! *(90 minutes)*

Welcome: WAGi Cheer! *(5 minutes)*

[As kids arrive, gather in a circle for the WAGi Cheer. Hold up the WAGi Cheer poster. Chant and do the moves together!]

GUIDE:

It's lab day, WAGi Mates. I can't wait to hear all about how you've been practicing your detective skills! But first… it's time for the WAGi Cheer!

Wonder *(Arms out, palms up)*

Yes, AND *(Hi-five)*

Get Messy *(Both arms circle up & out in front of body)*

I Can *(Fist pump)*

WAGi!!!!!!

Flashback *(5 minutes)*

Goal: Reconnect kids with ideas and accomplishments from last lab experience

Skills: Curiosity, Connection, Listening, Compassion, Detective Skills

Needs: Kids' Neighborhood Maps, Lists of Good Things and Problems in the Neighborhood, Detective Skills Chart, Detective Questions List

[Be sure kids have the neighborhood maps that they made in the last session. Hold up the Detective Skills Chart.]

GUIDE:

Last time, we talked about these detective skills and made maps that show our neighborhoods! We also got a chance to be detectives with each other, and listed the good things and the problems we uncovered in our community.

Did any of you get to use the detective questions to do more neighborhood exploring with your friends or family?

[If kids had a chance to talk to others outside the lab, have them share what they learned. Add new ideas to the list. Congratulate those who extended their questioning beyond the lab.]

Getting Down to Basics *(30 minutes)*

Goal: Introduce the concept of needs, identifying basic needs and other needs

Skills: Connection, Uncovering Needs, Detective Skills

Needs: Kids' Neighborhood Maps, Kids' Neighborhood Needs List, Basic Needs Poster, Marker or Writing Tool

GUIDE:

We uncovered lots of information about our neighborhood. The good things make people happy. Let's figure out why!

[Choose a specific example of a good thing from the kids' lists or one of the maps, and suggest a need it fills, e.g., park gives kids a place to play, flowers make pollen for bees, farm provides food for community, a pool lets people escape the summer heat.

Challenge WAGi kids to tell why other things they listed or showed on their maps make people feel good or happy. What needs do they meet? Accept all ideas by responding Yes, AND! Offer suggestions when appropriate, and write the need(s) that are being met next to each list example.]

GUIDE:

Now, let's look at the problems we found that make people unhappy in their neighborhood. What makes people unhappy? You guessed it! When they don't have the things they need, or when there are dangers or they don't feel safe.

[Ask kids to choose problems or needs from their maps or lists. Ask why they make people feel badly. What needs are not being met? Again, accept all ideas, give suggestions, and write the needs on the maps or next to problems on the list.]

34

We've talked about many different needs. But only some of them are Basic Needs. Basic needs are the things we all need to survive - or keep living. Can you guess what they are?

[Get responses from kids before holding up the Basic Needs Poster. Then display the poster, and discuss why food is important. Do the same for clothing, shelter, and water. If kids have other suggestions, discuss them, and accept all opinions.]

GUIDE:

Now that we have thought about basic needs, let's go back to our list and maps. Which of the needs we added are basic needs?

[Review the list again and maps. Have kids circle the basic needs.]

GUIDE:

Once we know what people need, we can start to think about out how to help them. That is the biggest WAGiLab goal of all!

Brain Break! (Yoga) *(5 minutes)*

Goal: Give kids a chance to move and take a break from discussion activities.

GUIDE:

Let's try something different today - a yoga break! Yoga is great for stretching out your muscles and relaxing your body and your brain! C'mon, lab-sters! Do it with me!

[Have the kids stand up facing you. Be sure they have enough room so they won't bump into each other. Do this sequence of yoga poses. Movements can be accompanied by gentle music.

Video: https://www.youtube.com/watch?v=eCe6w_kUFik

1: Breath of Joy: Stand with legs apart. Swing arms forward, and then straight back behind you. Swing them forward and up next to your ears. Finally, swing them down and through your legs, and back up out in front of you. Breathe in with each arm extension, and exhale as arms swing through legs. Do this 10 times.

2: Side Swing Fling: Swing arms side to side, let them flop loosely while turning at the waist. Turn and look behind you with each arm swing. Repeat 10 times.

3: Tree Balance Challenge: End with this calming pose. Hold your hands together in front of your heart. Stand tall, holding your rear in and keeping your shoulders down. Lift one leg up and rest the sole of your foot on the inside of the other leg. Stand tall and try to hold the pose for one minute.

If kids have trouble balancing, let them stand next to a wall, desk or other support to complete this exercise. When they finish the Tree Balance, have them sit quietly in chairs or on the floor with their eyes closed for one minute.]

Uncovering Neighborhood Challenges *(30 minutes)*

Goal: Introduce the concept of needs, identifying basic needs and other needs

Skills: Connection, Uncovering Needs, Detective Skills

Needs: Mash-Up Poster, Kids' Neighborhood Maps and Lists of Good Things and Problems, Basic Needs Poster, Writing Paper, Markers or Writing Tools

[Display the Mash-Up Poster}

GUIDE:

Now we're going to play a game that I call "PPN Mash-Up." PPN stands for Places, Problems, and Needs. Mixing and matching these categories can help us think of new ideas and come up with possible needs in our neighborhood.

[Explain that to play, each team starts by rolling the die three times, and chooses the **PLACE** *that matches the first number, the* **PROBLEM** *that matches the second number, and the* **Need** *that Matches the third number. Point to the PPN poster and ask kids what their three mash-up components would be if they rolled a 2, 5, and 1.]*

[The Mash-Up: **Place = HOME; Problem = ACCIDENTS; Need = FOOD.***]*

Now let's "Mash-Up these three picks by filling in the sentence from the poster:

In a <u>HOME</u>, how can <u>ACCIDENTS</u> cause problems with <u>FOOD</u>, or keep people from getting the <u>FOOD</u> they need?

[As a group, brainstorm some challenging situations that might be caused by this "Mash-Up." If kids need help, suggest these examples or others:

- *If a milk container is carelessly left on the kitchen counter all day, the milk can go sour. If someone puts the container back in the fridge (not realizing that the milk is sour), another person might drink it and get sick.*

- *If a parent serves a dish made with peanuts at a birthday party, and forgets to ask if anyone is allergic to peanuts, there might be a serious problem if one of the guests has an allergic reaction to the nuts.*

After a few ideas have been discussed, have kids split up in teams of 3 or 4. Give each team a die and let kids play Mash Up with new numbers and components.]

GUIDE:

Now it's your turn. Roll the die three times to pick your Place, Problem, and Need. Imagine yourself in the place you picked in your neighborhood. Then think about the need and try to brainstorm how the problem might cause some challenging situations.

[Encourage kids to come up with real problems that exist in the neighborhood, or possible problems that might happen. Have them write down all of their ideas. After kids come up with 2 or 3 ideas about challenges to solve, roll again and get new ideas from the next "Mash-Up." After 15-20 minutes, bring kids together so they can share the results of the Mash-Up brainstorming. If kids have new ideas, add them to the lists.]

Wrap Up! *(5 minutes)*

Goals: Kids share thoughts about what they've explored and learned in the day's mission

Skills: Listening, Curiosity, Sharing, Connection

Needs: Basic Needs Poster, Mash-Up Poster and Ideas List, Kids' Neighborhood Maps and Lists of Good Things and Problems, Log Books

[Sit in a circle or close together with the Detective Skills Chart on display. Ask kids what they learned about being a detective. Was it easy to talk to their partners?]

GUIDE:

> Today, we explored basic needs and played a game to help us come up with new situations and needs in the neighborhood. What did you learn by playing Mash-Up? Did you come up with ideas that surprised you?
>
> Next time, we'll explore what it's like to walk in the shoes of others so we can understand what they see and how they feel.

Log In! *(5 minutes)*

Goals: Kids reflect further, and write or draw pictures in their personal logs to save their feelings, thoughts, and ideas about the "Uncovering Needs" Mission.

Skills: Reflection, Communicating ideas and feelings

Needs: Basic Needs Poster, Mash-Up Poster and Ideas List, Kids' Neighborhood Maps and Lists of Good Things and Problems, Log Books

[After LogBooks have been handed out to team members.]

GUIDE:

> Add some thoughts or pictures to tell or show what you learned and how this day made you feel.

[After kids have finished writing in their LogBooks, collect the books.]

WAGi High Five! *(1 minutes)*

GUIDE:

> We did a lot of detective work today, and have lots to think about! Right now, let's end with a big WAGi High Five.

[End with a reminder about the next WAGiLab meeting!]

Uncovering
Neighborhood Challenges

GOAL: To help kids use creative thinking to discover community needs.

PLACES

1. School

2. Home

3. Park/Playground

4. Shopping

5. Street

6. Hangout

PROBLEMS

1. Germs

2. Trash

3. Crime

4. Bullying

5. Accidents

6. Poverty

NEEDS

1. Food

2. Shelter

3. Water

4. Clothing

5. Good Health

6. Safety

www.wagilabs.org

INSTRUCTIONS:

Roll one die three times. First pick a **PLACE**, then pick a **PROBLEM** and finally, pick a **NEED**. "Mash-Up" your picks together by filling in your picks in this sentence:

"In a **PLACE**, how can **PROBLEM** cause problems with **NEED**, or keep people from getting the **NEED** they need?

Use the question to help you brainstorm needs in your community. After you get some ideas, roll again and get new ideas from the new "Mash-Up."

By trying on other people's shoes and walking in them, we can see life as they see it, and feel what they feel. That is called having EMPATHY. Having empathy is how we understand the changes that are needed in the world.

Let's try on shoes to see through others' eyes.

WAGiLabs Mission 4:

Walk in Others' Shoes! *(90 minutes)*

Welcome: WAGi Cheer! *(5 minutes)*

Goals: Kids reconnect and build sense of team by chanting the WAGi Cheer

Skills: Connection, Teamwork

Needs: WAGi Cheer Poster

[As kids arrive, gather in a circle for the WAGi Cheer. Hold up the WAGi Cheer poster. Chant and do the moves together!]

GUIDE:

It's lab day, WAGi Mates. I hope you've been practicing your detective skills! Now... it's time for the WAGi Cheer!

Wonder *(Arms out, palms up)*

Yes, AND *(Hi-five)*

Get Messy *(Both arms circle up & out in front of body)*

I Can *(Fist pump)*

WAGi!!!!!!

Flashback *(5 minutes)*

Goal: Reconnect kids with ideas and accomplishments from last lab experience

Skills: Curiosity, Connection, Listening, Compassion, Detective Skills

Needs: Detective Skills Chart, Questions List, Kids' Needs List, Basic Needs Poster

GUIDE:

Last time, we talked about basic needs and played a game to help us think about people's needs in new ways.

We've come up with a big list of needs, but how can we know the best ways to help? Today, we're going to look at things we can do to better understand how to help others.

42

Different Shoes, Different Views *(60 minutes)*

Goal: Practice walking in other people's shoes, develop empathy, identify needs

Skills: Imagination, Connection, Empathy, Uncovering Needs

Needs: Walk in Others' Shoes Poster, Act It Out! Poster, Age Simulation Suit video, marker or writing tool, Sticky Notes and Disability props:

1. Bucket or wastebasket (to hinder walking)
2. Eyeglasses smeared with Vaseline or other clear gel (to hinder vision)
3. Scarves or dish towels to use as slings (to disable an arm)
4. Backpack filled with books or heavy objects (to make movement more difficult)
5. Oversized winter gloves or mittens (to make hand actions difficult)

Part 1: Just Imagine *(10 minutes)*

[Sit in a circle. Hold up the Walk in Others' Shoes Poster.]

GUIDE:

Walk in Others' Shoes!

Today, we're going to think about a skill we can use to help us give others what they really need. It's called EMPATHY." When you have empathy you can "put yourself in someone else's shoes to see what they see or feel what they feel." You imagine how YOU would feel in the same situation.

Have you ever hurt your foot and had to use crutches like the one Wagi has on the poster? Suddenly, your favorite sneaker doesn't fit and you have to wear a cast when you walk. How does life change when your shoe changes?

[Prompt kids to think about what it's like to have a broken leg and walk with a cast. They might feel lopsided or off-balance with a shoe on one foot and a big cast on the other. They might have trouble getting out of bed, taking a shower, or getting dressed. It might be hard to walk, climb stairs, run on the playground, or keep up with their friends. Challenge kids to imagine themselves in different situations where a cast would make it more difficult to get around.]

43

Once a cast comes off, most people can run and jump and play just like before. But what if your cast never came off? What if you had to live with a broken leg for the rest of your life?

[Ask if kids know anyone who has a permanent disability, for example, someone with a leg, arm or back that doesn't work well or who uses a wheelchair because s/he can't walk at all. If kids don't think of it, remind them to consider people who can't see and can't hear. Explain that problems that affect how your body works are called disabilities.]

Part 2: Act It Out *(20 minutes)*

[Group kids in teams of 2 and display Act It Out! Poster]

GUIDE:

People who are very old might have any of the physical limits that we just talked about. Can you imagine what it would be like to live their lives? How would you feel?

[If you have access to the Internet, show the suggested video about the age simulation suit. https://www.theguardian.com/society/video/2014/mar/31/age-simulation-suit-healthcare-old-video . If not, go directly to the activity.

Let each team choose one of the props to explore what life might be like with a disability:

- *Walking with one foot in a bucket or wastebasket simulates having an injured foot*

- *Wearing Vaseline-covered glasses simulates having poor vision*

- *Wearing a sling simulates having a non-functioning arm*

- *Wearing a weighted backpack simulates having a back or movement problem*

- *Wearing oversized gloves simulates having problems with hands and fingers]*

GUIDE:

Let's all walk in the shoes of older people. Use the props to help you imagine the situations you might face each day. What kinds of problems might you have? How would your life be different?

44

[Pass out the Day in the Life Posters, and challenge teammates to act out activities old people might do at each time during the day, and come up with 10 problems they might face.

Have kids write their ideas, thoughts and feelings about older people's daily lives on sticky notes and place them on the poster next to the appropriate times. If kids need help, suggest specific activities like getting dressed, doing food shopping, getting to a doctor's appointment, cooking dinner, etc.

Also fill in the time on the clock faces. After 15 minutes, bring the whole group together to share thoughts and combine them in a list.]

Brain Break! (Blindfolds) *(10 minutes)*

Goal: Give kids a chance to further explore physical disabilities.

Skills: Be active, move, empathy

Needs: Blindfolds

Prep: Set up a simple obstacle course on the floor of the lab using plastic bottles or containers.

[Set up the obstacle course in the room. Keep kids paired up, and hand out a blindfold to each team.]

GUIDE:

We've started exploring what it's like to have a disability, let's keep going.

[Have kids take turns being blindfolded while their partner leads them through the obstacle course by first giving verbal instructions, then, holding their hand and giving physical guidance. What did kids experience? Which way was it more difficult to move through the course, using spoken directions or physical guidance? Can they imagine what it would be like to be blind all of the time?]

Part 3: From First Steps to Next Steps *(30 minutes)*

Goal: Practice walking in other people's shoes, develop empathy, identify needs

Skills: Imagination, Connection, Empathy, Uncovering Needs

Needs: Walk in Others' Shoes Poster, List of Old People's Problems, Voting Dots

GUIDE:

Now that we have been imagining what it's like to have some of

the problems that older people do, and seeing things from their point of view, we can start to think of ways we can help. First, let's choose the problems we think are most important.

[Call kids up by team. Have each team member put 3 blue dots on the most important problem, two blue dots on the second most important, and one blue dot on the third important problem. When all WAGi kids have voted, count the dots and create a separate "TOP FIVE LIST" of problems faced by older people. Be sure to leave space between items in the list so there is room to add ways to help for each one.]

GUIDE:

Having imagined what it's like for older people to live with these five important problems, what are some ways we could help them?

[Encourage all ideas, and add them below each problem on the list. Respond to each suggestion with "Yes, AND..." Try to focus on one problem at a time, and be sure to get several responses related to each of the five problems.]

Extra Activity: Walk in People's Shoes Cards

Goal: Practice walking in other people's shoes, develop empathy, identify needs

Skills: Imagination, Connection, Empathy, Uncovering Needs

Needs: Walk in Others' Shoes Cut Up Cards, Shoe Box

GUIDE:

People in need of help aren't just people who can't walk or run. So let's try on other people's' shoes in our imagination. Maybe some shoes are stinky. Other shoes might be fancy. Some might have no laces. Some people might not have any shoes at all.

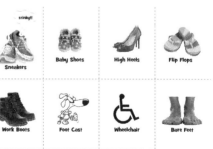

[Child picks a shoe cut-out from out of a shoe box. On back of the cut-out shoe is a story describing the situation that the wearer of the shoes is in. The kids then describe how the shoe wearer must be feeling and suggest ways to help them.]

Walk in Others' Shoes! Cut-Outs

Wrap Up! *(5 minutes)*

Goals: Kids share thoughts about what they've learned in the day's mission

Skills: Imagination, Connection, Sharing, Empathy, Uncovering Needs

Needs: Walk in Others' Shoes Poster, Day in the Life Poster, List of Old People's Problems, Log Books

[Sit in a circle or close together with the Walk in Others' Shoes Poster on display. Ask kids what they learned about walking in someone elses' shoes.]

GUIDE:

Alright! You did a great job showing empathy as you tried on other peoples' shoes! How did imagining what life with physical problems is like help you understand the needs older people might have? Did you discover anything that surprised you?

Empathy is how we understand the changes that are needed in the world. In our next session we will use our new empathy skills to look at the needs in our neighborhood and try to understand how we can help with those needs.

Log In! *(5 minutes)*

Goals: Kids reflect further, and write or draw pictures in their personal logs to save their feelings, thoughts, and ideas about the Walk in Others' Shoes Mission.

Skills: Reflection, Communicating ideas and feelings

Needs: Detective Question List, Walk Shoes Poster, Log Books

[After LogBooks have been handed out to team members.]

GUIDE:

Add some thoughts or pictures to tell or show what you learned about walking in other people's shoes and having empathy, and how this day made you feel.

[After kids have finished writing in their LogBooks, collect the books.]

WAGi High Five! *(1 minutes)*

We did a lot of detective work today, and have lots to think about! Right now, I think we need to end with a big WAGi High Five.

[End with a reminder about the next WAGiLab meeting!]

Walk in Others' Shoes!

Flip Flops

Bare Feet

High Heels

Foot Cast

Baby Shoes

stinky!!

Sneakers

Work Boots

Act It Out!

Injured Foot

Poor Vision

**Non Functioning
Arm**

**Back
Problems**

**Hand/Fingers
Problems**

Day in the Life of _____

Walk in another person's shoes for a day and record the time on the clock faces and their activities on sticky notes and place them along the pathway.

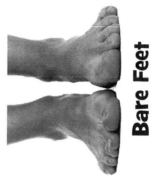

Flip Flops

Bare Feet

High Heels

Wheelchair

Baby Shoes

Foot Cast

stinky!!

Sneakers

Work Boots

Walk in Others' Shoes! Cut-Outs

It's time to team up, talk together, and decide which needs we want to work on. Wagi Mate teams evaluate our list of neighborhood needs, and pick one need to tackle.

WAGiLabs Mission 5:

Team Up! *(90 minutes)*

Welcome: WAGi Cheer! *(5 minutes)*

Goals: Kids reconnect and build sense of team by chanting the WAGi Cheer

Skills: Connection, Teamwork

Needs: WAGi Cheer Poster

[As kids arrive, gather in a circle for the WAGi Cheer. Hold up the WAGi Cheer poster. Chant and do the moves together!]

GUIDE:

It's lab day, WAGi Mates. Now... it's time for the WAGi Cheer!

Wonder *(Arms out, palms up)*

Yes, AND *(Hi-five)*

Get Messy *(Both arms circle up & out in front of body)*

I Can *(Fist pump)*

WAGi!!!!!!

Flashback *(5 minutes)*

Goal: Reconnect kids with ideas and accomplishments from last lab experience

Skills: Curiosity, Connection, Listening, Compassion, Detective Skills

Needs: Detective Skills Chart, Questions List, Kids' Needs List, Basic Needs Poster

GUIDE:

Last time, we talked about walking in other people's shoes and thinking about how you would feel if you were living each person's life. Do you remember any needs we talked about – any that might make someone's life very hard?

[Hold up the Walk Shoes Poster]

Today, we get a chance to be detectives again. We're going take a closer look at our lists of neighborhood needs and use our new empathy skills to better understand how those needs affect people's lives.

[Hold up the Needs Lists]

Before we do, does anyone have new needs to add to our lists?

[Guide the conversation about the neighborhood. Add new ideas to the list. Congratulate those who extended their questioning beyond the lab.]

Voting to Help *(60 minutes)*

Goal: Introduce the concept of needs, identifying basic needs and other needs, developing empathy

Skills: Curiosity, Connection, Uncovering Needs, Compassion, Detective Skills

Needs: Kids' Needs Lists, Basic Needs Poster, Team Up! Poster, paper for kids to write on, markers or writing tools

Prep: Post the Needs Lists on the wall or in a place where all kids can see them

GUIDE:

We all came to the WAGiLab to help make people's lives better. Now, it's time to choose the special needs and problems that we want to work on. Let's take a closer look at our lists.

We uncovered many needs in our neighborhood. Which needs do you think are most important? Each WAGi Mate gets five votes . When it's your turn, put a check mark next to the 5 needs you would like to help on. After everyone votes, we will tally up the checks to find our choices for the top need areas in our neighborhood.

[Have kids take turns "checking" their favorite needs. After everyone has voted, count the votes and highlight or circle the 5 most popular needs.]

Now we're going to split up into three teams.

[Have kids count off by threes, i.e., 1-2-3, 1-2-3, etc. Group all kids with the same number on a team. Be sure kids have paper and writing tools so they can write down their top need choices.]

Okay, teams, it's up to you to talk together and decide which top needs you want to work on. Pick one from the neighborhood list. Write it down.

Let's start by asking who in the neighborhood has this need? Imagine walking in the shoes of that person - or group of people so you can better understand how they feel.

Take 5 minutes to talk with your teammates about how someone in the shoes would define the need, or tell others about it. Write down your ideas.

Then ask more questions to help you think about the people with the need or problem. Ask:

- Do the people want help with the need?
- How would they make the situation better if they had the resources?
- Has anyone tried to work to make the need better?
- How would we help people or our neighborhood by filling this need?

Sometimes, walking in different shoes can give you more thoughts about how we can help people. Can you think of another pair of shoes to try on to give you more ideas about your neighborhood need?

[Help kids come up with different approaches. For example, if the need is for clean water because a nearby river or lake is polluted, kids might put on the shoes of kids who want to swim, people who want to protect the environment or animals, or fishermen who want to catch fish. Make sure the kids capture their thoughts on a whiteboard or on paper.]

Brain Break-Dance! *(5 minutes)*

Goal: Give kids a chance to get active and take a break from discussion activities.

Skills: Be active, move

Needs: Music CDs and player or streamed music from the WAGiLab Playlist

[Guide jumps up, shakes, moves arms, etc.]

GUIDE:

Woohoo! I think I need a chance to be in my own shoes – for a dancing breakdance! C'mon, lab-ster, get down and move!

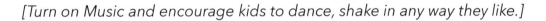

[Turn on Music and encourage kids to dance, shake in any way they like.]

Wrap Up! *(5 minutes)*

Goals: Kids share thoughts about what they've learned in the day's mission

Skills: Listening, Curiosity, Sharing, Connection

Needs: Detective Skills Chart, Basic Needs Chart, Walk Shoes Poster, Log Books

[Sit in a circle or close together with the Walk Shoes Poster on display. Ask kids what they learned about walking in someone elses' shoes.]

GUIDE:

Let's talk about the detective work we did today. Did the questions you asked help you understand the needs of our neighborhood and world. What did you learn about the people who have these needs? Did you discover anything that surprised you?

Log In! *(5 minutes)*

Goals: Kids reflect further, and write or draw pictures in their personal logs to save their feelings, thoughts, and ideas about the Walk in Others' Shoes Mission.

Skills: Reflection, Communicating ideas and feelings

Needs: Detective Question List, Walk Shoes Poster, Log Books

[After LogBooks have been handed out to team members.]

GUIDE:

Add some thoughts or pictures to tell or show what you learned and how this day made you feel.

[After kids have finished writing in their LogBooks, collect the books.]

WAGi High Five! *(1 minutes)*

GUIDE:

We did a lot of detective work today, and have lots to think about! Right now, I think we need to end by walking in our own shoes and giving a big WAGi High Five.

[End with a reminder about the next WAGiLab meeting!]

Team Up!

1.

Vote for 5 Needs

2.

Form 3 Teams

3.

Walk in Neighborhood's Shoes

4.

Ask Questions???

Define Challenge!

Defining a challenge means thinking about problems and goals. How can we look at our need as a challenge that we want to solve?

Let's find out!

WAGiLabs Mission 6:
Define Challenge *(90 minutes)*

Welcome: WAGi Cheer! *(5 minutes)*

Goals: Kids reconnect and build sense of team by chanting the WAGi Cheer

Skills: Connection, Teamwork

Needs: WAGi Cheer Poster

[As kids arrive, gather in a circle for the WAGi Cheer. Hold up the WAGi Cheer poster. Chant and do the moves together!]

GUIDE:

It's lab day, WAGi Mates. Now... it's time for the WAGi Cheer!

Wonder *(Arms out, palms up)*

Yes, AND *(Hi-five)*

Get Messy *(Both arms circle up & out in front of body)*

I Can *(Fist pump)*

WAGi!!!!!!

Flashback *(5 minutes)*

Goal: Reconnect kids with ideas and accomplishments from last lab experience

Skills: Curiosity, Connection, Listening, Compassion, Detective Skills

Needs: Detective Skills Chart, Questions List, Kids' Needs List, Basic Needs Poster

GUIDE:

Last time, we teamed up and walked in other people's shoes to explore the needs we want to help fill. We now get a chance to be detectives again. We want to look at our need as a challenge that we want to solve. To do that we have to define the challenge.

Beginning with the End in Mind *(60 minutes)*

Goal: Introduce the concept of seeing the future solution and working backwards

Skills: Curiosity, Connection, Uncovering Needs, Detective Skills

Needs: Kids' Needs List, Basic Needs Poster, marker or writing tool

GUIDE:

To build a home, a carpenter begins with blueprints. To make a cake, a baker starts with a recipe. Beginning with the end in mind involves imagination – the ability to envision your future.

In problem solving, you envision the future by asking what do you want to accomplish when we fill this need? So the first question that we want our team to answer is to begin with the end in mind by asking:

What is the result we want to achieve in solving this need?

To practice this question: Let's imagine there has been an earthquake and people need to get first aid but there's a big crack in the earth between them and the hospital. What is the result we want to achieve?

Define Wagi's Challenge

1. WHAT is the result we want to achieve?
2. WHY do we want to achieve this result?

[Show Define Poster. Have kids capture their thoughts and write out an answer.]

Now onto the second question. **Why** is the most often asked question by kids.

Why is the sky blue?

Why do I have to brush my teeth?

Why?

We ask Why? 65 times per day. Sometimes a why question can be very serious, like why did you get out of bed this morning? Why did you?

[Have kids answer this get out of bed question.]

GUIDE:

Those are great reasons to get out of bed. I especially like to make it a better world. So now answer this why question.

Why do we want to achieve the result you just described in question #1?

[Have kids capture their thoughts and write out an answer.]

Now from your answers to the What and Why questions you can write out the definition of your challenge of getting to the hospital.

[Have kids write out the definition of this earthquake challenge.]

Let's apply what we just learned to our define the neighborhood challenge that we picked from Mission #5.

What is the result we want to achieve in solving this need?

[Have kids capture their thoughts and write out an answer.]

Why do we want to achieve this result you just described in filling this need?

[Have kids capture their thoughts and write out an answer.]

Now from your answers to the What and Why questions you can write out the definition of your challenge for the neighborhood.

[Have kids capture their thoughts and write out an answer.]

The definition of your challenge will lead us to our next session called Brainstorm Solutions.

Brain Break! *(5 minutes)*

Goal: Give kids a chance to get active and take a break from discussion activities.

Skills: Be active, move

Needs: Music CDs and music player or streamed music from the WAGiLab Playlist

GUIDE:

C'mon, lab-ster, get up and move!

[Turn on Music and encourage kids to get moving in any way they like.]

Wrap Up! *(5 minutes)*

Goals: Kids share thoughts about what they've learned in the day's mission

Skills: Listening, Curiosity, Sharing, Connection

Needs: Define Poster, Log Books

[Sit in a circle. Ask kids what they learned from asking what and why questions?]

GUIDE:

Let's talk about the detective work we did today. Did the questions you asked help you define your challenge? Did you discover anything that surprised you?

Log In! *(5 minutes)*

Goals: Kids reflect further, and write or draw pictures in their personal logs to save their feelings, thoughts, and ideas about the Define Challenge Mission.

Skills: Reflection, Communicating ideas and feelings

Needs: Define Poster, Log Books

[After LogBooks have been handed out to team members.]

Add some thoughts or pictures to tell or show what you learned and how this day made you feel.

[After kids have finished writing in their LogBooks, collect the books.]

WAGi High Five! *(1 minute)*

We did a lot of detective work today, and have lots to think about! Right now, we need to end with a big WAGi High Five.

[End with a reminder about the next WAGiLab meeting!]

Define Wagi's Challenge

1. WHAT is the result we want to achieve?

2. WHY do we want to achieve this result?

Brainstorm Solutions

Get ready to put on your thinking cap. On our first Brainstorming Day, everyone gets to share lots and lots of ideas - and no one says "NO!"

On our second Brainstorming Day, we stretch our minds to see what's good about our ideas, and come up with our wildest ideas yet!

WAGiLabs Mission 7:

Brainstorm Solutions

DAY ONE *(90 minutes)*

Welcome: WAGi Cheer! *(5 minutes)*

Goals: Kids reconnect and build sense of team by chanting the WAGi Cheer

Skills: Connection, Teamwork

Needs: WAGi Cheer Poster

[As kids arrive, gather in a circle for the WAGi Cheer. Hold up the WAGi Cheer poster. Chant and do the moves together!]

GUIDE:

It's lab day, WAGi Mates. It's time for the WAGi Cheer!

Wonder *(Arms out, palms up)*

Yes, AND *(Hi-five)*

Get Messy *(Both arms circle up & out in front of body)*

I Can *(Fist pump)*

WAGi!!!!!!

> Wonder
> Yes, AND
> Get Messy
> I can
> WAGi!!!
>
> www.wagilabs.org

Flashback *(5 minutes)*

Goal: Reconnect kids with ideas and accomplishments from last lab experience

Skills: Curiosity, Connection, Listening, Compassion, Detective Skills

You will need: Detective Skills Chart, Define Wagi's/Your Challenge Poster

GUIDE:

Last time, we learned how to clearly describe a challenge, and used What and Why questions to learn more about the needs we chose. Up 'til now, we've acted like detectives: uncovering needs and walking in other peoples' shoes.

Get ready for more fun because we are going to walk in the

shoes of a Brainstormer. That's someone who creates exciting ideas to fill the needs we have uncovered and defined.

You'll learn new questions to go along with Yes, AND! You'll learn What if?, Why not? and What would we never do?

Voila... What a Great Idea! *(60 minutes)*

Goal: Introduce the concept of brainstorming

Skills: Curiosity, Connection, Uncovering Needs, Detective Skills

Needs: Kids' Needs List, Basic Needs Poster, World Map, each team's Challenge Definition, Brainstorming Poster, Brainstorming Rules Poster, Wagi's Challenge Poster, large pads or construction paper for ideas, marker or writing tools

What a Great Idea! PART 1

[Hold up What's a Brainstorm? Poster]

GUIDE:

Have you ever heard the word "brainstorm?" What do you think it means?

What's a Brainstorm?

[Have kids try to define it. Encourage them to think about the two smaller words within the word "brainstorm" as they suggestion definitions.]

When we "Brainstorm," we let all our creative ideas flow out, like swirling winds in a storm. Brain-Storm, get it? No idea is too big or too small; everyone gets to share lots of ideas. Are you ready to start?

[After kids respond, have them break into their small teams. Give each team a pad or piece of paper, a writing tool, and the challenge definition from last session.]

Our steps for brainstorming are simple:

Step 1: Agree on your challenge... you already did that! So, copy your team's challenge definition at the top of your big sheet of paper.

[Wait for kids to write their definitions.]

Now comes the fun...

Step 2: Coming up with ideas. Just like we asked detective questions to help us uncover needs, we can ask special brainstorming questions to help us think of ideas to solve the challenge.

[Show the Brainstorm Poster.]

Our three brainstorm questions are:

1. What if...

2. Why is this a good idea?

3. What would we never do?

We'll start with "What if?"

When you begin your idea with "What if..." you are trying to imagine ways to solve the need or problem.

[Show Wagi's Challenge Poster and the related challenge definition.]

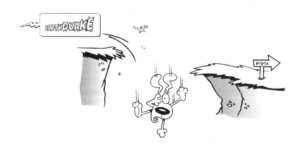

Remember Wagi's earthquake challenge? I have one idea that that might solve it... What if... giant trucks filled the crack with rocks so the ambulance could drive over the rocks to the hospital? That's only one possible solution. Can you think of other ways we might solve the problem? Start your idea with "What if…"

[Get a few ideas from team members. Remind kids to accept all ideas, and together, say "Yes, AND" after each one.]

GUIDE:

Yeah! You're getting it! So, let's use the "What if" question to come up with ideas to solve your challenges! Work together as a team to come up with at least ten ideas.

[Pull out the Brainstorming Rules Poster.]

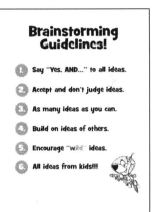

Follow these simple Brainstorming guidelines:

1. Say "Yes, AND" to all ideas.

2. Accept everything. Don't judge!

3. Think of as many ideas as you can.

4. Encourage wild and wacky ideas.

5. Build on the ideas of others.

6. Be sure all ideas come from kids! No adults allowed!!!

Please capture your ideas on sticky notes and put them all over a poster board or a wall.

[Give teams 30 minutes to come up with ideas. Walk around and encourage everyone to share. After teams have come up with at least 8-10 ideas, take a Brain Break.]

Brain Break! *(5 minutes)*

Goal: Give kids a chance to get active and take a break from discussion activities.

Skills: Be active, move

Needs: Music CDs and music player or streamed music from Playlist on our website

[Guide jumps up, shakes, moves arms, etc.]

GUIDE:

Woohoo! You've been working hard on those ideas. I think we all need to get up and take a break! C'mon, lab-ster, let's move!

[Turn on Music and encourage kids to get moving in any way they like.]

Wrap Up! *(5 minutes)*

Goals: Kids share thoughts about what they've learned in the day's mission
Skills: Listening, Curiosity, Sharing, Connection
Needs: Possibility Poster, Log Books

[Sit in a circle or close together with the Brainstorm Poster on display. Ask kids what they learned from asking what if and why not and never questions.]

GUIDE:

Let's talk about the ideas we created today. Did the questions you asked help you come up with ideas to solve your challenge? Did other WAGi teammates have ideas that gave you new ideas? Did you discover anything that surprised you?

Log In! *(5 minutes)*

Goals: Kids reflect further, and write or draw pictures in their personal logs to save their feelings, thoughts, and ideas about the Brainstorming Mission.

Skills: Reflection, Communicating ideas and feelings

Needs: Brainstorm Poster, Log Books

WAGi High Five! *(1 minute)*

GUIDE:

We did a lot of detective work today, and have lots to think about! Right now, I think we need to end with a big WAGi High Five.

[End with a reminder about the next WAGiLab meeting!]

72

WAGiLabs Mission 7:

Brainstorm Solutions

DAY TWO *(90 minutes)*

Welcome: WAGi Cheer! *(5 minutes)*

Goals: Kids reconnect and build sense of team by chanting the WAGi Cheer

Skills: Connection, Teamwork

Needs: WAGi Cheer Poster

[As kids arrive, gather in a circle for the WAGi Cheer. Hold up the WAGi Cheer poster. Chant and do the moves together!]

GUIDE:

It's lab day, WAGi Mates. It's time for the WAGi Cheer!

Wonder *(Arms out, palms up)*

Yes, AND *(Hi-five)*

Get Messy *(Both arms circle up & out in front of body)*

I Can *(Fist pump)*

WAGi!!!!!!

Flashback *(5 minutes)*

Goal: Reconnect kids with ideas and accomplishments from last lab experience

Skills: Curiosity, Connection, Listening, Compassion, Detective Skills

You will need: Detective Skills Chart, Define Wagi's/Your Challenge Poster

GUIDE:

Last time, we learned how to ask the question "What if..." to help us come up with ideas to solve our challenge. We are again going to walk in the shoes of a Brainstormer and ask new questions.

Voila... What a Great Idea! *(60 minutes)*

Goal: Introduce the concept of brainstorming

Skills: Curiosity, Connection, Uncovering Needs, Detective Skills

Needs: Kids' Needs List, Basic Needs Poster, World Map, each team's Challenge Definition, Brainstorming Poster, Brainstorming Rules Poster, Wagi's Challenge Poster, large pads or construction paper for ideas, marker or writing tools

Why is it Good? *(25 minutes)*

GUIDE:

Alright! Let's get back to our idea lists. Now that you have lots of possible solutions for your challenge, the next step is to look at your list again.

Transfer your list of ideas to the Ideas Poster. Then for each idea, ask yourself: "Why is it good?" See if you can think of ways that each idea might help you solve the problem and write them down.

[Remind kids to talk only about what they like – and not to talk about reasons ideas might not work. Remind them to take notes.]

NeverNever Land! *(35 minutes)*

GUIDE:

Our brainstorming doesn't stop here. We need to stretch our brains and come up with some wild ideas that might even surprise us! To do this, ask yourself: What would we "never" do to solve our challenge? Be silly. Be wacky! Make a list of 5-10 things you would never do to solve the problem.

[Now, challenge kids to look again at their wild and impossible ideas, and see if they can find ways to make them possible.]

So, you think that you'd never do those last ideas, right? Well, I've got one final brainstorming challenge! Look at your "never" ideas, and see if you can think of a way to turn a

74

"No way!" idea into a "Great way!" idea.

Twist it, turn it, combine it with another idea, or change it in any way to make it a good idea that CAN help solve your challenge! Be sure to write down all of your ideas.

[Walk around the lab. Offer help if kids need it. Suggest ways to look at an idea differently or combine it with other ideas to make it work.]

Congratulations, Labsters! You have just completed your first brainstorm! You came up with lots of ideas. Do you think all of them will work? Probably not!

Next time, we'll look more closely at our ideas, and decide which ones might help us reach our goal, and which ones won't work as well OR might not work at all! That's called giving and Getting Feedback.

Brain Break *(5 minutes)*

Goal: Give kids a chance to get active and take a break from discussion activities.

Skills: Be active, move

Needs: Music CDs and music player or streamed music from Playlist on our website

[Guide jumps up, shakes, moves arms, etc.]

GUIDE:

Woohoo! You've been working hard on those ideas. I think we all need to get up and take a break! C'mon, lab-ster, let's move!

[Turn on Music and encourage kids to get moving in any way they like.]

Wrap Up! *(5 minutes)*

Goals: Kids share thoughts about what they've learned in the day's mission

Skills: Listening, Curiosity, Sharing, Connection

Needs: Possibility Poster, Log Books

[Sit in a circle or close together with the Brainstorm Poster on display. Ask kids what they learned from asking what if and why not and never questions.]

GUIDE:

Let's talk about the ideas we created today. Did the questions you asked help you come up with ideas to solve your challenge? Did other WAGi teammates have ideas that gave you new ideas? Did you discover anything that surprised you?

Log In! *(5-10 minutes)*

Goals: Kids reflect further, and write or draw pictures in their personal logs to save their feelings, thoughts, and ideas about the Brainstorming Mission.

Skills: Reflection, Communicating ideas and feelings

Needs: Brainstorm Poster, Log Books

[After LogBooks have been handed out to team members.]

GUIDE:

Add some thoughts or pictures to tell or show what you learned about brainstorming, some of your ideas for solutions, and how this day made you feel.

[After kids have finished writing in their LogBooks, collect the books.]

WAGi High Five! *(1 minute)*

GUIDE:

We did a lot of brainstorming today, and have lots of ideas to think about! Right now, I have one more idea, let's end with a big WAGi High Five!

[End with a reminder about the next WAGiLab meeting!]

Brainstorming Questions

Brainstorming Guidelines!

1. Say "Yes, AND..." to all ideas.

2. Accept and don't judge ideas.

3. As many ideas as you can.

4. Build on ideas of others.

5. Encourage "wild" ideas.

6. All ideas from kids!!!

1.	**1.**
2.	**2.**
3.	**3.**
4.	**4.**
5.	**5.**
6.	**6.**
7.	**7.**
8.	**8.**
9.	**9.**
10.	**10.**

Brainstorm ideas to help solve your challenge. Write them all down. No judging. Then ask "Why is the idea good?" and write down your responses.

1.	1.
2.	2.
3.	3.
4.	4.
5.	5.
6.	6.
7.	7.
8.	8.
9.	9.
10.	10.

Think of a way to turn a "No way!" idea into a "Great way!" idea. Twist it. Flip it. Combine it with another idea to make it a GREAT idea that CAN solve your challenge!

Feedback from others helps us improve our ideas and build the confidence to make them real.

Let's reach out to others to learn what they think!

WAGiLabs Mission 8:

Get Feedback *(90 minutes)*

Welcome: WAGi Cheer! *(5 minutes)*

Goals: Kids reconnect and build sense of team by chanting the WAGi Cheer

Skills: Connection, Teamwork

Needs: WAGi Cheer Poster

[As kids arrive, gather in a circle for the WAGi Cheer. Hold up the WAGi Cheer poster.]

GUIDE:

It's lab day, WAGi Mates. Now... it's time for the WAGi Cheer!

Wonder *(Arms out, palms up)*

Yes, AND *(Hi-five)*

Get Messy *(Both arms circle up & out in front of body)*

I Can *(Fist pump)*

WAGi!!!!!!

Flashback *(5 minutes)*

Goal: Reconnect kids with ideas and accomplishments from last lab experience

Skills: Curiosity, Connection, Listening, Compassion, Detective Skills

Needs: Detective Skills Chart, Brainstorm Poster

GUIDE:

Last time, we learned how to walk in the shoes of a Brainstormer and create exciting ideas by asking three questions: "What if?", "What makes it good?" and "What would we never do?"

Now it's time to get feedback about our ideas. Feedback helps us look more closely at ideas, improve them, and even say "NO" to ideas that will never work.

Here's My Opinion! Part 1 *(30 minutes)*

Goal: Introduce the concept of getting constructive feedback

Skills: Curiosity, Connection, Uncovering Needs, Detective Skills

Needs: Ideas List, Feedback Loop Poster, marker or writing tool

When you put your heart into creating an idea, it can be hard to judge whether the idea is good, great or just OK! Getting comments from other people can help you think about your idea and make it better. Comments and other feedback can also give you confidence to keep going so you can turn your idea into reality.

The "Get Feedback" Loop

[Show Get Feedback Loop Poster]

If you show your idea to your friends and family, it's easy for them to simply say that it's nice. If you want to get more honest feedback and suggestions, the best way is to ask specific questions like these:

1. Does our idea make sense to you? Do you think it could work? If not, what could we do to make it work?

2. Do you understand our idea? Is there anything you don't understand? If so, how can we make our idea clearer? Do we need to know anything else to better understand our idea?

3. What are the things you like the most about our idea?

4. If this was your idea, how would you change it?

5. Do you think you can make this idea happen? Why or why not?

83

Now it's time to present our ideas to each other and get feedback. Of course, if everyone likes our ideas, we'll be happy. But, don't feel badly if some feedback sounds critical or negative. Remember, the comments are about the ideas, not about you! More importantly, as every inventor learns, negative comments can help you make your idea better.

So, Team 1, you're up first! Tell everyone about your ideas. Then, ask two questions from the list to get feedback from your friends.

[Remind the kids on Team 1 to write down all suggestions, and to thank their Wagi Mates for their ideas. After Team 1 has gotten feedback, have Team 2 and then Team 3 present and take notes.]

GUIDE:

Great job, Teams!!

Here's My Opinion! Part 2 *(30 minutes)*

GUIDE:

You've all gotten lots of feedback. Some suggestions will help your team improve your ideas. But, you don't have to use all of the feedback. If your team disagrees with comments, it's OK. You can keep your idea the way you presented it.

So, take 5 minutes to talk about the feedback, and see if you can use it to improve your idea. If the feedback helps you know that some ideas won't work, now's the time to "let go" of them.

Brain Break! *(5 minutes)*

Goal: Give kids a chance to get active and take a break from discussion activities.

Skills: Be active, move

Needs: Music CDs and music player or streamed music from Playlist on our website

[Guide jumps up, shakes, moves arms, etc.]

GUIDE:

Since our brains have been working so hard on those ideas, let's give our bodies a workout, too!! C'mon, Wagi Mates, let's get up and take a break!

[Turn on Music and encourage kids to get moving in any way they like.]

Wrap Up! *(5 minutes)*

Goals: Kids share thoughts about what they've learned in the day's mission

Skills: Listening, Curiosity, Sharing, Connection

Needs: Get Feedback Poster, Log Books

[Sit in a circle or close together with the Feedback Poster on display. Ask kids what they learned from getting feedback?]

GUIDE:

Let's talk about the feedback we received today. Did the feedback help you improve upon your ideas? Did you discover anything that surprised you?

Log In! *(5 minutes)*

Goals: Kids reflect further, and write or draw pictures in their personal logs to save their feelings, thoughts, and ideas about the Get Feedback Mission.

Skills: Reflection, Communicating ideas and feelings

Needs: Feedback Poster, Log Books

[After LogBooks have been handed out to team members.]

GUIDE:

Add some thoughts or pictures to tell or show what you learned and how this day made you feel.

[After kids have finished writing in their LogBooks, collect the books.]

WAGi High Five! *(1 minute)*

We did a lot of detective work today, and have lots to think about! Right now, I think we need to end with a big WAGi High Five.

[End with a reminder about the next WAGiLab meeting!]

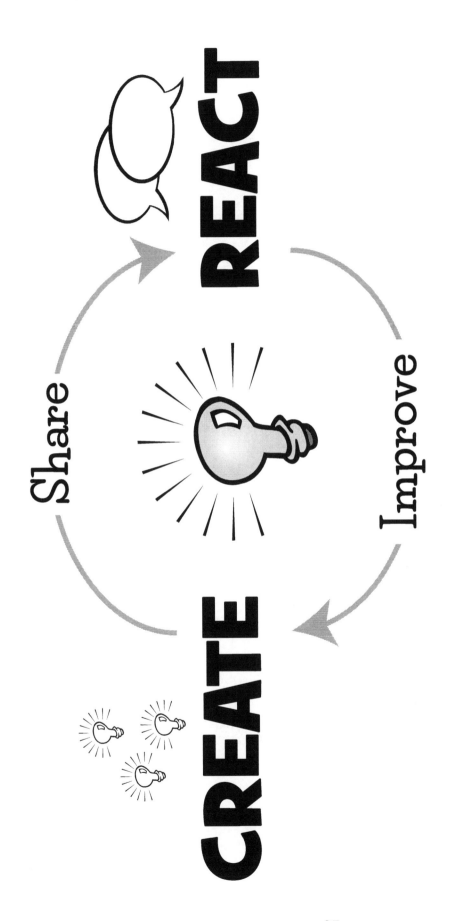

REACT

Share

Improve

CREATE

The "Get Feedback" Loop

Build Prototypes

Now that we have ideas, it is time to experiment with possible solutions. On Day One, we build models or prototypes of possible solutions, and share them with others to see how they work.

On Day Two, we test if our prototypes work? Are there problems? Do we have to make changes? Through the ups and downs of the inventing process, we learn that persistence and resilience are keys to turning our ideas into action. We don't give up!

WAGiLabs Mission 9:
Build Prototypes
DAY ONE *(90 minutes)*

Welcome: WAGi Cheer! *(5 minutes)*

Goals: Kids reconnect and build sense of team by chanting the WAGi Cheer

Skills: Connection, Teamwork

Needs: WAGi Cheer Poster

[As kids arrive, gather in a circle for the WAGi Cheer. Hold up the WAGi Cheer poster.]

GUIDE:

It's lab day, WAGi Mates. It's time for the WAGi Cheer!

Wonder *(Arms out, palms up)*

Yes, AND *(Hi-five)*

Get Messy *(Both arms circle up & out in front of body)*

I Can *(Fist pump)*

WAGi!!!!!!

Flashback *(5 minutes)*

Goals: Reconnect kids with ideas and accomplishments from last lab experience

Skills: Curiosity, Connection, Listening

Needs: Detective Skills Chart, Brainstorm Poster, Feedback Poster, Feedback Notes

GUIDE:

Last time, we learned how to ask questions to get feedback. Then, we listened to feedback comments and used them to make our ideas better. How did you feel about getting feedback? How did it help you improve your ideas?

Today, we are going to learn how to build prototypes of our ideas so we can get even more feedback.

Playing with Prototypes, Part 1 *(60 minutes)*

Goal: Introduce the concept of creating a model or prototype for an idea

Skills: Brainstorming, Teamwork, Creative & Critical Thinking

Needs: Challenge Definitions, Prototype Steps Poster, "Stop Germs" Poster, Idea Lists, markers or writing tools, building materials for prototypes; 3 empty boxes or bins, one for each Team (to store building materials)

Prep: Set up lab space to allow for building. Gather the materials kids will use to make prototypes. Organize the building materials in labeled boxes or bins. Here are some materials (feel free to add others):

Clay	Play Doh
Fabric	Buttons
Cardboard	Magazines
Picture and Shape Stickers	Yarn/String
Pipe Cleaners	Rubber Bands
Craft Sticks/Popsicle Sticks	Scissors
Craft Foam Sheets	Paper Clips
Recycled Plastic Containers	Duct Tape
Recycled Boxes	Glue
Paper/Plastic Cups	Velcro
LEGO or other snap-together blocks	Markers
Paper towel and toilet paper rolls	Chopsticks

GUIDE:

A prototype is a model that shows your idea. Some prototypes show what your idea looks like. Others demonstrate how your idea works. Best of all, once you make a prototype, you can show it to others to get more feedback to improve your idea.

Here are examples of prototypes designed to help kids stop spreading cold germs.

1. Which ideas do you like best?

2. Which ones would kids have to build?

3. Which could they do by drawing?

4. Do some of the parts look familiar?

5. Did any parts come from products that already exist?

[Show the "Stop Germs" Poster, talk about elements used to make each model. Are they from other products, made from scratch, a combination?

When you finish discussing the Germs Poster examples, take out the Prototype Steps Poster.]

GUIDE:

Now, it's time for each team to design and build a prototype to show off your idea. Just like you saw on the "Stop Germs" Poster, there are lots of ways to do it.

Sometimes, you can just draw your prototype. Other times, you might have to build it. You can build a prototype from scratch – which means you make every part, or, you can find pieces from products that already exist, and put them together. It all depends on your idea!

[Hold up the Prototype Steps Poster.]

GUIDE:

Here is a list of steps to follow as you build your prototype.

Let's start with Step 1.

Work together with your teammates to draw a picture of the prototype you want to build. Talk about the parts, and choose one person to draw as you talk.

Try to think about all of the parts you'll need. If a full-size prototype is too big to build, you can build a small model that looks like the final big one.

Prototype Steps

☐ Draw a detailed sketch of your idea. Plan carefully. Include all of the parts that make it work.

☐ When your sketch is finished, check out the materials you have to work with in your WAGiLab. What can you use to build each part? Make a list of the materials you will need.

☐ Finally, make a list of the jobs your team members will need to do to build the prototype. Decide who will do each job. You can work together on jobs, too!

☐ Gather the materials you are going to use. Keep them neatly organized so you can find each one when you need it.

☐ Build your prototype!! If you are going to draw your final prototype, start drawing!

☐ At any time, if you are not happy with your prototype, change it! If some of your pieces don't work, try different pieces, or different ways to make each part.

☐ If your prototype doesn't work out, you might have to change your idea or make a new prototype. Don't give up! It's all part of the invention process!

[Explain Step 2 on the Prototype Steps Poster. Walk around the lab and answer questions that the WAGI kids have. Feel free to suggest ideas about possible materials to use or part resources to get kids thinking creatively. After kids have made their lists of materials, they might need help listing and dividing up the tasks.]

Now that your sketch is finished, Step 2 is to check out the materials you have to work with in your WAGiLab. What can you use to build each part?

Make a list of the materials you will need.

[Walk around the lab and help kids create their materials lists.]

Now that you made your materials list, Step 3 is to think about the different tasks involved in creating a prototype. Are there different things you need to build? Are there parts that need pictures or words? Look at each part of your prototype and decide how it will get made.

Make a list of the jobs your team members will need to do to build the prototype. Decide who will do each job. You can work together on jobs, too.

[Walk around the lab and help kids create their task lists, and then assign tasks. After finishing the lists, take a Move It! Break.]

Brain Break! *(5 minutes)*

Goal: Give kids a chance to get active and take a break from discussion activities.

Skills: Be active, move

Needs: Music CDs and music player or streamed music from Playlist on our website

[Jump up, shake your arms, start dancing, etc.]

We are not done making our prototypes, don't worry, we'll complete them tomorrow. Let's now get up and shake out the creaks in our bones! C'mon, show me how you move!

Wrap Up! *(5 minutes)*

Goals: Kids share thoughts about what they've learned in the day's mission

Skills: Listening, Curiosity, Sharing, Connection

Needs: Get Feedback Poster, Log Books

GUIDE:

Wow. Today was an amazing day! You worked on your very first prototypes! What was it like? Did you find the right materials? Did you have to make any changes to the parts? How did your team work together? Was it easy? Did each of you find it easy do your job? Did you run into any problems? Next session, we'll finish our prototypes.

Log In! *(5 minutes)*

Goals: Kids reflect further, and write or draw pictures in their personal logs to save their feelings, thoughts, and ideas about the Build Prototypes Mission.

Skills: Reflection, Communicating ideas and feelings

Needs: Prototype Steps Poster, Prototypes, Log Books

[After Log Books have been handed out to team members.]

GUIDE:

Before we end, take some time to write in your log books! Add some thoughts or pictures to tell or show what you learned today as you and your team worked on your prototype. Tell how this day made you feel.

[After kids have finished writing in their Log Books, collect the books.]

WAGi High Five! *(1 minute)*

GUIDE:

We did a lot of building today, and have lots to think about! Right now, I think we need to end with a big WAGi High Five.

[End with a reminder about the next WAGiLab meeting!]

STOP
Germs!

Our uncovered need is to reduce spreading cold germs among elementary school kids? Big Need!!!

Prototype Examples:

1. They could build a prototype of a really fun facemark they could wear when they have a cold and are contagious.

2. They could create a socially "viral" animation that shows how germs spread when you sneeze or don't wash your hands.

3. They could create a cool way to carry sanitary wipes and pass out new wipes when kids are in need.

4. They could teach kids to sing a song while washing your hands so you know when you have washed long enough.

Ideas require different types of prototypes: from building a workable mockup, to storyboarding the end product, to creating a song or posters for display in classrooms.

Prototype Steps

- ☐ Draw a detailed sketch of your idea. Plan carefully. Include all of the parts that make it work.

- ☐ When your sketch is finished, check out the materials you have to work with in your WAGiLab. What can you use to build each part? Make a list of the materials you will need.

- ☐ Finally, make a list of the jobs your team members will need to do to build the prototype. Decide who will do each job. You can work together on jobs, too!

- ☐ Gather the materials you are going to use. Keep them neatly organized so you can find each one when you need it.

- ☐ Build your prototype!! If you are going to draw your final prototype, start drawing!

- ☐ At any time, if you are not happy with your prototype, change it! If some of your pieces don't work, try different pieces, or different ways to make each part.

- ☐ If your prototype doesn't work out, you might have to change your idea or make a new prototype. Don't give up! It's all part of the invention process!

WAGiLabs Mission 9:

Build Prototypes

DAY TWO *(90 minutes)*

Welcome: WAGi Cheer! *(5 minutes)*

Goals: Kids reconnect and build sense of team by chanting the WAGi Cheer

Skills: Connection, Teamwork

Needs: WAGi Cheer Poster

[As kids arrive, gather in a circle for the WAGi Cheer. Hold up the WAGi Cheer poster. Chant and do the moves together!]

GUIDE:

It's lab day, WAGi Mates. Now… it's time for the WAGi Cheer!

Wonder *(Arms out, palms up)*

Yes, AND *(Hi-five)*

Get Messy *(Both arms circle up & out in front of body)*

I Can *(Fist pump)*

WAGi!!!!!!

Flashback *(5 minutes)*

Goals: Reconnect kids with ideas and accomplishments from last lab experience

Skills: Curiosity, Connection, Listening

Needs: Detective Skills Chart, Brainstorm Poster, Feedback Poster, Feedback Notes

GUIDE:

Last time, we started building our prototypes of our idea. Today, we are going to finish building our prototypes and present them to the class to get their feedback.

Playing with Prototypes Part 2 *(30 minutes)*

Goal: Introduce the concept of creating a model or prototype for an idea

Skills: Brainstorming, Teamwork, Creative & Critical Thinking

Needs: Challenge Definitions, Prototype Steps Poster, "Stop Germs" Poster, Idea Lists, markers or writing tools, building materials for prototypes; 3 empty boxes or bins, one for each Team (to store building materials)

Prep: Set up lab space to allow for building. Gather the materials kids will use to make prototypes. Organize the building materials in labeled boxes or bins. Here are some materials (feel free to add others):

Clay	Play Doh
Fabric	Buttons
Cardboard	Magazines
Picture and Shape Stickers	Yarn/String
Pipe Cleaners	Rubber Bands
Craft Sticks/Popsicle Sticks	Scissors
Craft Foam Sheets	Paper Clips
Recycled Plastic Containers	Duct Tape
Recycled Boxes	Glue
Paper/Plastic Cups	Velcro
LEGO or other snap-together blocks	Markers
Paper towel and toilet paper rolls	Chopsticks

[Give each team a labeled storage box or bin for their building materials.]

GUIDE:

It's time to gather the materials you'll need for your prototype and start building! Remember, work together and ask each other questions as you build.

At any time, if you are not happy with your prototype, change it! If some of your pieces don't work, try different pieces, or different ways to make each part.

If your prototype doesn't work out, you might have to change your idea or make a new prototype. Don't give up! It's all part of the invention process!

[Teams work on prototypes. Offer help and suggestions as needed. Encourage kids to work together to clean up the lab. Remind them: If you mess up, you have to clean up!]

Presenting your Prototypes *(30 minutes)*

Goal: Presenting your prototypes to the class for feedback

Skills: Teamwork, Presenting, Listening

Needs: Prototype, Feedback questions List

GUIDE:

Now it's time to present our prototypes to each other and get feedback. Of course, if everyone likes our ideas, we'll be happy. But, don't feel badly if some feedback sounds critical or negative. Even negative comments can help you make your idea better.

So, Team 1, you're up first! Tell everyone about your prototype. Then, ask at least two of the following questions to get feedback from your friends:

1. Do you understand our idea? Is there anything you don't understand? If so, how can we make our idea clearer?

2. What are the things you like the most about our idea?

3. If this was your idea, how would you change it?

4. Do you think we can make this idea happen? Why or why not?

[Remind the kids on Team 1 to write down all suggestions, and to thank their Wagi Pals for their ideas. After Team 1 has gotten feedback, have Team 2 and then Team 3 present and take notes.]

GUIDE:

Great job, Teams!!

You've all gotten lots of feedback. Some suggestions will help your team improve your ideas. But, you don't have to use all of the feedback. If your team disagrees with comments, it's OK. You can keep your idea the way you presented it.

So, take 5 minutes to talk about the feedback, and see if you can use it to improve your idea. If the feedback helps you know that some ideas won't work, now's the time to "let go" of them.

Brain Break! *(5 minutes)*

Goal: Give kids a chance to get active and take a break from discussion activities.

Skills: Be active, move

Needs: Music CDs and music player or streamed music from Playlist on our website

[Jump up, shake your arms, start dancing, etc.]

Wrap Up! *(5 minutes)*

Goals: Kids share thoughts about what they've learned in the day's mission

Skills: Listening, Curiosity, Sharing, Connection

Needs: Get Feedback Poster, Log Books

GUIDE:

Wow. You presented your very first prototypes! What was it like? Did you have to make any changes to the prototypes after receiving the feedback?

How did your team work together? Did you run into any problems?

Log In! *(5 minutes)*

Goals: Kids reflect further, and write or draw pictures in their personal logs to save their feelings, thoughts, and ideas about the Build Prototypes Mission.

Skills: Reflection, Communicating ideas and feelings

Needs: Prototype Steps Poster, Prototypes, Log Books

[After Log Books have been handed out to team members.]

GUIDE:

Before we end, take some time to write in your log books! Add some thoughts or pictures to tell or show what you learned today as you and your team worked on your prototype. Tell how this day made you feel.

[After kids have finished writing in their Log Books, collect the books.]

WAGi High Five! *(1 minute)*

GUIDE:

We did a lot of building today, and have lots to think about! Right now, I think we need to end with a big WAGi High Five.

[End with a reminder about the next WAGiLab meeting!]

What's the best way to present your ideas to your class, parents, teachers, members of the community? A perfect pitch, of course.

Let's learn how to tell a story that makes our ideas irresistable!

Plan Your Pitch *(90 minutes)*

Welcome: WAGi Cheer! *(5 minutes)*

Goals: Kids reconnect and build sense of team by chanting the WAGi Cheer.

Skills: Connection, Teamwork

Needs: WAGi Cheer Poster

[As kids arrive, gather in a circle for the WAGi Cheer. Hold up the WAGi Cheer poster.]

GUIDE:

It's lab day, WAGi Mates. Let's start with the WAGi Cheer!

Wonder *(Arms out, palms up)*

Yes, AND *(Hi-five)*

Get Messy *(Both arms circle up & out in front of body)*

I Can *(Fist pump)*

WAGi!!!!!!

Flashback *(5 minutes)*

Goal: Reconnect kids with ideas and accomplishments from last lab experience

Skills: Curiosity, Connection, Listening, Compassion, Creative & Critical Thinking, Detective Skills

Needs: Detective Skills Chart, Brainstorm Poster, Feedback Poster

GUIDE:

Last time, we worked on building prototypes to show and test our ideas. If your prototype isn't quite done, we'll try to set aside time so you can do more work later. Right now, each team is going to create a plan to pitch your idea.

Make a Storyboard! *(40 minutes)*

Goal: Introduce concepts of storyboarding and pitching ideas

Skills: Curiosity, Connection, Uncovering Needs, Storytelling, Drawing, Logical Thinking, Detective Skills

Needs: Storyboard Pix Poster, Storyboard Steps Poster, Ideas List, Challenge Definition, Teams' Prototypes, Sticky Notes, Magazines for Pictures, Scissors, Markers or Writing Tools

Prep: Cut out different ads from magazines (for food, tech products, kids' products, restaurants, travel spots, etc.). Gather magazines for kids to use as picture resources.

GUIDE:

A pitch is a way to get people excited about your idea or solution. It's kind of like a TV commercial or an ad in a magazine!

[Take out the magazine ads you've clipped. Ask kids to choose the ones they like best. Why do they like each one? Which ads don't they like? Why?]

GUIDE:

A good ad or TV commercial makes you want to buy something (like a new phone or video game) or do something (go to McDonald's or the movie Star Wars). A good pitch does the same thing. It tells a story about why your solution is GREAT, and makes people want to "buy" or support your idea.

[Show Storyboarding Your Idea Poster]

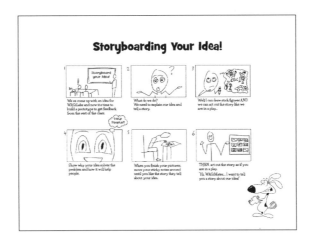

Now, it's time to make a storyboard to plan your pitch. A storyboard has pictures that tell the story of your idea. You decide what comes first, next, and at every step - until you end with a big BANG!

[Explain how kids can draw pictures by doodling to tell a story about their idea and show how it solves their challenge.]

What shapes are used for this picture?

[Then go over the first part of the Storyboard Steps Poster to be sure kids know what information to include in their storyboard. Before moving on to the 4 steps, hand out sticky pads and drawing tools.]

Let's start by deciding what comes first, next, and last in your story.

Think how your ideas would be shown in a TV commercial or in a movie. What would the first scene of your story be?

Sketch it out on "sticky notes." You can draw stick figures or cut out pictures from magazines.

Then move on to the next scene... and the next scene. You can show drawings, photos, anything that will help people understand your idea.

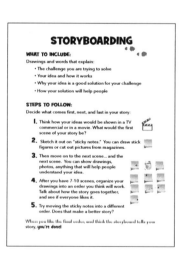

104

After you have 7-10 scenes, organize your drawings into an order you think will work. Talk about how the story goes together, and see if everyone likes it.

[Read the first step aloud, and then let kids start. Walk around and answer any questions kids have about the process or steps. When all teams have their first drawing finished, encourage them to continue making more pictures for their storyboards.

As kids work, remind them to check the Storyboard Steps Poster to be sure that they have included all of the important information about their idea.

After about 15 minutes (or sooner, if kids are moving quickly), give a 10-minute warning. When time's up, introduce Step 3 on the Steps Poster.]

GUIDE:

Now it's time to look at all of your sticky notes. Are they in the right order? Talk about them together, and move them around if you want. When you think your storyboard tells the story of your idea in a way that will make everyone "buy" it, you're done!!

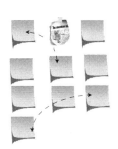

[Let kids play with their storyboard notes. Encourage them to move the parts around, to try their idea "story" in different ways. If Team members realize that they have missed a step, they can create new sticky notes and add them. When all teams are happy with their storyboards, take a Move It! break!]

Brain Break! *(5 minutes)*

Goal: Give kids a chance to get active and take a break from discussion activities.

Skills: Be active, move

Needs: Music CDs and music player or streamed music from Playlist on our website.

[Jump up, shake your body, wiggle your arms, etc.]

GUIDE:

Woohoo! You've been working hard on those storyboards. I think we all need to get up and take a break! C'mon, lab-sters, let's move!

[Turn on the Music and encourage kids to get moving in any way they like.]

Practice Your Story Pitch! *(20 minutes)*

Goal: Let kids practice using a storyboard to pitch an idea; reinforce the idea of getting feedback and using feedback to make pitch or storyboard revisions

Skills: Curiosity, Connection, Uncovering Needs, Storytelling, Drawing, Logical Thinking, Detective Skills

Needs: Storyboard Your Idea Poster, Storyboard Steps Poster, Ideas List, Challenge Definition, Teams' Prototypes, Sticky Notes, Magazines for Pictures, Scissors, Markers or Writing Tools

GUIDE:

Okay, teams, it's time to practice your idea pitches. Team 1, you're up first! Using your storyboard, tell everyone the story of your idea. Don't forget to talk about your prototype!

[After Team 1 presents, have members from the listening teams give feedback, using the Feedback Questions from Mission 7:

1. *Did the story pitch make sense?*

2. *Did they understand the idea and think it could work?*

3. *Were there any things that they didn't understand?*

4. *Do they have suggestions or ideas about changes for the pitch?*

Be sure Team 1 members take notes about the feedback. Then have Teams 2 and 3 present their idea pitches and get feedback.]

GUIDE:

Congratulations! You did your first storyboard pitches and got lots of feedback! Now take some time to use the feedback to improve your storyboard pitch or your idea. Remember, sometimes comments that sound negative can help you the most!

Now is also the time to "let go" of parts of your idea that might not work. If you think your whole idea won't work, that's okay. You can pick another idea and go in a totally different direction. In the idea world, we call this "pivoting."

Wrap Up! *(5 minutes)*

Goals: Kids share thoughts about what they've learned in the day's mission

Skills: Listening, Curiosity, Sharing, Connection, Summarizing

Needs: Storyboard Poster, Storyboards, Prototypes, Log Books

[Sit in a circle or close together with the Storyboard Poster on display. Ask kids what they learned from getting feedback.]

GUIDE:

Let's talk about our day. Did making a storyboard help you explain your idea? What did you learn when you told your story to other WAGi Mates? Did you get feedback that helped you improve your idea? Did you discover anything that surprised you? Did any of you "pivot" and choose another idea?

Next time when we get together, you'll get a chance to expand your storyboard so you can pitch your idea to new people at the Guppy Tank.

Log In! *(5 minutes)*

Goals: Kids reflect further, and write or draw pictures in their personal logs to save their feelings, thoughts, and ideas about the Build Prototype Mission.

Skills: Reflection, Communicating ideas and feelings

Needs: Storyboard Posters, Storyboards, Prototypes, Log Books

[After Log Books have been handed out to team members.]

GUIDE:

Add some thoughts or pictures to tell or show what you learned today as you and your team made a storyboard and practiced your pitch. Tell how this day made you feel.

[After kids have finished writing in their Log Books, collect the books.]

WAGi High Five! *(1 minute)*

GUIDE:

What a day! You made storyboards, practiced your idea pitches, and made changes based on the feedback you got! Let's celebrate our day with a big WAGi High Five.

[End with a reminder about the next WAGiLab meeting!]

Doodling 101

Line ————

Rectangle

Triangle

Oval

Squiggle

Cartoons only have four fingers.

what shapes are used for this picture?

Storyboarding Your Idea!

1

Storyboard your Idea!

We've come up with an idea for WAGiLabs and now it's time to build a prototype to get feedback from the rest of the class.

2

What do we do?
We need to explain our idea and tell a story.

3

Well I can draw stick figures AND we can act out the story like we are in a play...

4

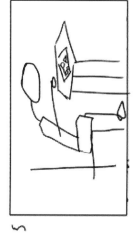

Help People!!!

Show why your idea solves the problem and how it will help people.

5

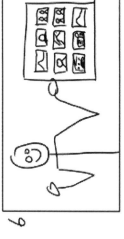

When you finish your pictures, move your sticky notes around until you like the story they tell about your idea.

6

THEN, act out the story as if you are in a play.

"Hi, WAGiMates... I want to tell you a story about our idea!"

STORYBOARDING

WHAT TO INCLUDE:

Drawings and words that explain:

- The challenge you are trying to solve
- Your idea and how it works
- Why your idea is a good solution for your challenge
- How your solution will help people

STEPS TO FOLLOW:

Decide what comes first, next, and last in your story:

1. Think how your ideas would be shown in a TV commercial or in a movie. What would the first scene of your story be?

2. Sketch it out on "sticky notes." You can draw stick figures or cut out pictures from magazines.

3. Then move on to the next scene... and the next scene. You can show drawings, photos, anything that will help people understand your idea.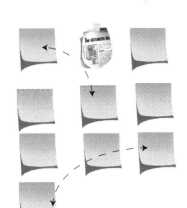

4. After you have 7-10 scenes, organize your drawings into an order you think will work. Talk about how the story goes together, and see if everyone likes it.

5. Try moving the sticky notes into a different order. Does that make a better story?

When you like the final order, and think the storyboard tells your story, **you're done!**

Practice! Practice! Practice!

WAGiLabs Mission 11:

GuppyTank Practice

DAY ONE *(90 minutes)*

Welcome: WAGi Cheer! *(5 minutes)*

Goals: Kids reconnect and build sense of team by chanting the WAGi Cheer

Skills: Connection, Teamwork

Needs: WAGi Cheer Poster

[As kids arrive, gather in a circle for the WAGi Cheer. Hold up the WAGi Cheer poster. Chant and do the moves together!]

GUIDE:

It's lab day, WAGi Mates. It's time for the WAGi Cheer!

Wonder *(Arms out, palms up)*

Yes, AND *(Hi-five)*

Get Messy *(Both arms circle up & out in front of body)*

I Can *(Fist pump)*

WAGi!!!!!!

Flashback *(5 minutes)*

Goal: Reconnect kids with ideas and accomplishments from last lab experience

Skills: Curiosity, Connection, Listening, Compassion, Detective Skills

Needs: Storyboard Poster, Brainstorm Poster

GUIDE:

Last time, we created our first storyboards to pitch our ideas. Now, it's time to make our stories even better so we can pitch our ideas at the Guppy Tank!

Once Upon a Time... *(40 minutes)*

Goal: To learn how to present (pitch) your ideas to an audience of parents, teachers, members of your community.

Skills: Curiosity, Connection, Uncovering Needs, Storytelling, Detective Skills

Needs: Idea Prototypes, Team Storyboards, Storytelling Outline Poster, one copy of the Storytelling Poster for each Team, Stop Germs Poster, Show Time Poster, Idea ScoreCard Poster, marker or writing Tool.

Prep: Print out one copy of the Storytelling Outline for each team.

GUIDE

The Guppy Tank is where you'll get to present your ideas to lots of people, not only kids from our WAGiLab. When you tell your idea story at the Guppy Tank, you want to go over the top, and act it out to make your audience really like it!

[Ask kids to take out their storyboards.]

GUIDE:

Remember last time, we said that pitches were like TV commercials? For the Guppy Tank, you're going to stretch your storyboard stories - by thinking of them as movies instead of just commercials!! That means bigger AND better!

[Take out the Storytelling and Stop Germs Posters.]

GUIDE:

Let's talk more about storytelling. Have you seen the movies Toy Story or Finding Nemo? Stories like this, especially fairy tales, often start out with these three words: "Once upon a time..."

[Point out Step 1 on the Storytelling Poster "Once upon a time..,". Explain that this phrase starts a story in a very personal way by introducing the main characters, what their life is like, or where the story takes place.

Give an example: "Once upon a time, there were three bears who lived in the forest: Papa Bear, Mama Bear and Baby Bear." The fairy tale for this one is pretty obvious!

114

Hold up the Stop Germs Story Poster. Ask a WAGi Mate to read the "Once Upon a Time…" introduction out loud. Then ask: Who are the characters in this Pitch Story? After you get the answer, continue.]

GUIDE:

Right! The characters in this Guppy Tank story are the kids in school who keep getting colds. The storyteller cares about the people, and wants you to care, too!

Now, it's your turn. Work with your teammates to write the introduction to your pitch story for your defined challenge. Tell who has the problem in a way that makes us care about them.

[Hand out the Storytelling Starters to each team. Suggest that kids can refer to their storyboards for reminders. Offer help as needed. When teams are ready, introduce the second outline step.]

GUIDE:

Now that we know the people or characters in your pitch story, it's time to tell about their problem. Let's look at the "Stop Germs" Story Pitch again.

[Hold up the poster and ask a WAGi Mate to read part 2 of the story.]

GUIDE:

Did you see how the storywriters made the problem sound dramatic? The more exciting your pitch is, the more people will get into it – just like an exciting movie.

Imagine acting out your pitch as you write. Tell about the challenge or problem you are trying to solve and how you found out about it. Start with the words "Every day…" Or, if the problem only happens sometimes, you might use the words "Every time…" Be dramatic!

[Give teams time to add info that tells about the problem or challenge they found. Walk around the room and offer help if needed. Remind kids to make their stories sound dramatic. Next, move on to step 3, introducing your idea or problem solution.]

Here comes the best part of your story - the big idea! You want everyone to know your solution to the problem, how you thought of it, and why it's such a great idea!

[Refer to the Stop Germs pitch, and ask how the big idea is introduced.

- *The pitch explains that thinking about Halloween masks helped the team come up with their solution. Since everyone knows about Halloween Masks, it's a great way to make their story personal.*
- *The pitch also mentions that when kids said they would only wear masks that were "cool," the team used that feedback to improve their idea to sticker masks.*
- *Finally, the pitch includes showing off 2 prototypes, an early "boring" one and improved "cool" one with stickers.]*

Sharing prototypes and telling how you used the feedback to make your idea better shows that you are working hard to design the best solution. It's a great way impress the Guppy Tank judges!

[Challenge kids to continue creating their pitch by telling how they came up with their idea, talking about one or more prototypes, and explaining how they used feedback to make their idea and/or prototype better.

Next move on to outline steps 4 and 5, having kids tell how their solution solves the problem - and why it's such a great idea for everyone.]

Brain Break! *(5 minutes)*

Goal: Give kids a chance to get active and take a break from pitch activities.

Skills: Be active, move

Needs: Music CDs and music player or streamed music from Playlist on our website

[Guide jumps up, shakes, moves arms, etc.]

You're really getting into your pitches. But now, let's get into some moving! Stand up and dance to the music!

[Turn on Music and encourage kids to get moving in any way they like.]

Sell It with a Slogan or a Song! *(20 minutes)*

Goal: Practice creating short, powerful pitches to sell ideas

Skills: Storytelling, Simplifying Ideas

Needs: Idea Prototypes, Each Team's Completed Outline Poster and Storyboard, markers or writing tools.

GUIDE:

A slogan is a catchy saying that tells about your idea. The shorter the better. A slogan can help you sell your idea – and help people remember it. The slogan for the Stop Germs pitch is: "Don't share your sneeze! Mask it, please!"

Take 10 minutes to come up with a short slogan for your idea. Make it fun and catchy so people will remember it.

If you have time left over, see if you can come up with a song about your idea, too! Or, work on a song instead of a slogan.

Wrap Up! *(5 minutes)*

Goals: Kids share thoughts about what they've learned in the day's mission

Skills: Listening, Curiosity, Sharing, Connection, Summarizing

Needs: StoryTelling Outline Poster, Storyboards, Prototypes, Log Books

[Sit in a circle or close together with the StoryTe;ing Outline Poster on display. Ask kids what they learned from storytelling.]

GUIDE:

Wow! Today was filled with storytelling. What was your favorite part of the day? Did the Storytelling Starters help you tell a more personal story about your idea?

Log In! *(5 minutes)*

Goals: Kids reflect further, and write or draw pictures in their personal logs to save their feelings, thoughts, and ideas about the GuppyTank Mission.

Skills: Reflection, Communicating ideas and feelings

Needs: Log Books

[After LogBooks have been handed out to team members.]

GUIDE:

Add some thoughts or pictures to your log book to tell or show what you learned and how this day made you feel. If you came up with a slogan for your idea, you might want to include it.

[After kids have finished writing in their LogBooks, collect the books.]

WAGi High Five! *(1 minute)*

GUIDE:

What a day! You made storyboards, practiced your idea pitches, and made changes based on the feedback you got! Let's celebrate our day with a big WAGi High Five.

[End with a reminder about the next WAGiLab meeting!]

[NOTE: Preparing for the Guppy Tank is one of the most important WAGiLab Missions. If you run out of time, feel free to extend your Lab to a second day so kids can finish all of the activities. Most importantly, be sure kids have time to practice their Guppy Tank pitches using the stories, prototypes, billboards, and slogans they have created.]

WAGiLabs Mission 11:

GuppyTank Practice

DAY TWO *(90 minutes)*

Welcome: WAGi Cheer! *(5 minutes)*

Goals: Kids reconnect and build sense of team by chanting the WAGi Cheer

Skills: Connection, Teamwork

Needs: WAGi Cheer Poster

[As kids arrive, gather in a circle for the WAGi Cheer. Hold up the WAGi Cheer poster. Chant and do the moves together!]

GUIDE:

It's lab day, WAGi Mates. It's time for the WAGi Cheer!

Wonder *(Arms out, palms up)*

Yes, AND *(Hi-five)*

Get Messy *(Both arms circle up & out in front of body)*

I Can *(Fist pump)*

WAGi!!!!!!

Flashback *(5 minutes)*

Goal: Reconnect kids with ideas and accomplishments from last lab experience

Skills: Curiosity, Connection, Listening, Compassion, Detective Skills

Needs: Storyboard Poster, Brainstorm Poster

GUIDE:

You made storyboards, practiced your idea pitches, and made changes based on the feedback you got! Now it's time to learn a new presentation method called Idea Billboarding.

Idea Billboard *(30 minutes)*

Goal: Practice creating short, powerful pitches to sell ideas

Skills: Storytelling, Simplifying Ideas

Needs: Idea Prototypes, Each Team's Completed Starter Poster and Storyboard, Billboard Poster, poster board or large pieces of paper, markers or writing tools.

Imagine that you're riding in a car and see a giant roadside billboard or giant poster on a building. Can you read it in 30 seconds and know what it is about? You bet! That's because billboards have big, bold pictures and very few words. They're designed to capture your attention in a flash before you pass.

Here's a billboard that we created for our WAGiLabs idea.

[Hold up Billboard Poster. Talk about the Call to Action, simple picture, and how the design breaks the rules by having part of the picture coming over the billboard border.]

WAGi Mates, it's time to create a billboard sign that tells the world about your idea. Follow these four guidelines:

1. Have a Call to Action (a challenge to others to help make your idea happen).

2. Use 10 words or less!

3. Use a simple picture to show your idea.

4. Break the rules.

Now make your billboard unforgettable!

Brain Break! *(5 minutes)*

Goal: Give kids a chance to get active and take a break from pitch activities.

Skills: Be active, move

Needs: Music CDs and music player or streamed music from Playlist on our website

[Guide jumps up, shakes, moves arms, etc.]

GUIDE:

You're really getting into your pitches. But now, let's get into some moving! Stand up, move your hips, and dance to the music!

[Turn on Music and encourage kids to get moving in any way they like.]

Pitching Practice! *(30 minutes)*

Goal: To learn how to present (pitch) your ideas to an audience of parents, teachers, members of your community.

Skills: Curiosity, Connection, Uncovering Needs, Storytelling, Detective Skills

Needs: Idea Prototypes, Each Team's Completed Starter Poster and Storyboard, GuppyTank Pitch Checklist, Show Time Poster, Idea ScoreCard Poster, marker or writing Tool.

GUIDE:

Just like you practiced your storyboard stories, you need to practice your Guppy Tank pitches to make them better. Let's try it now.

Here's a hint: Pretend that you're telling your best friends about your idea. Don't just read your notes; tell a story. Move around. Get excited about your prototype. If you're excited, other people will be excited!

At the Guppy Tank, people want to hear great ideas. Your pitch can convince them that your idea is great!

[Give kids a chance to practice. Walk around and suggest that they take turns and/or each tell a different part of the story. Remind them not to read the words. Encourage them to be energetic.]

Wrap Up! *(5 minutes)*

Goals: Kids share thoughts about what they've learned in the day's mission

Skills: Listening, Curiosity, Sharing, Connection, Summarizing

Needs: Team Story Pitches, Prototypes, Billboards, Slogans, Log Books

[Sit in a circle or close together with the Storytelling Starter and Billboard Poster on display. Ask kids what they learned from getting feedback.]

GUIDE:

How do you feel about your pitch? Do you think you need more practice before presenting at the Guppy Tank?

We'll be scheduling a time for the Guppy Tank soon so you can tell new people about your idea. Getting their feedback will help you take the next steps towards bringing your ideas to life!

Log In! *(5 minutes)*

Goals: Kids reflect further, and write or draw pictures in their personal logs to save their feelings, thoughts, and ideas about the GuppyTank Mission.

Skills: Reflection, Communicating ideas and feelings

Needs: Log Books

[After LogBooks have been handed out to team members.]

GUIDE:

Add some thoughts or pictures to your log book to tell or show what you learned and how this day made you feel. If you came up with a slogan for your idea, you might want to include it.

[After kids have finished writing in their LogBooks, collect the books.]

WAGi High Five! *(1 minute)*

What a day! You made storyboards, practiced your idea pitches, and made changes based on the feedback you got! Let's celebrate our day with a big WAGi High Five.

[End with a reminder about the next WAGiLab meeting!]

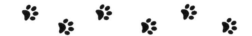

Storytelling Outline:

1. Once Upon a time...

Tell who has the problem, where they are, what life is like now.

2. And every day...

Tell what the problem is and how you found out about it.

3. Until one day...

Tell about your idea, how you came up with it, how you have made it better.

4. Because of that...

Tell how your ideas solves the problem.

5. Until finally...

Tell how people can help and what life will be like after the problem is solved.

Storytelling Starters:

> Once upon a time...

1. Once Upon a time...

2. And every day...

3. Until one day...

4. Because of that...

5. Until finally...

Sell your idea on an outdoor billboard!

Less words the better... Show, don't tell... Simple layout... Call to action... Break the rules

It's Show Time – time to celebrate and share the hard work of our WAGiLab teams. Kids have used detective skills to uncover needs in our community. They used brainstorming skills to come up with ideas to help solve those needs.

Now it's time to present our ideas and solutions to our panel of coaches who will help turn these ideas into reality.

WAGiLabs Mission 12:

Go Go GuppyTank *(90 minutes)*

Welcome: WAGi Cheer for All! *(5 minutes)*

Goals: Kids and guests connect and build sense of team by chanting the WAGi Cheer

Skills: Connection, Teamwork

Needs: WAGi Cheer Poster

[As kids arrive, gather in a circle for the WAGi Cheer. Hold up the WAGi Cheer poster.]

GUIDE:

Alright! Today's the big day! You're going to do your Guppy Tank pitches! That deserves a giant WAGi Cheer!

Wonder *(Arms out, palms up)*

Yes, AND *(Hi-five)*

Get Messy *(Both arms circle up & out in front of body)*

I Can *(Fist pump)*

WAGi!!!!!!

Flashback *(5 minutes)*

Goal: Reconnect kids with ideas and accomplishments from last lab experience

Skills: Curiosity, Connection, Listening, Storytelling, Creating Pitches to Present Ideas

Needs: Team Idea Storyboards and Pitch Stories

GUIDE

Last time, you used storytelling tips to make your idea pitch more exciting, and came up with catchy billboards and slogans to sell your idea. Today your hard work will pay off. It's Guppy Tank day!

Our Coaches Panel *(5 minutes)*

[Introduce the coaches to the kids and the kids to the coaches.]

GUIDE:

Welcome everyone. We are celebrating today the hard work of our WAGiLab teams. They have used their detective skills to uncover some needs in our community. They then used their brainstorming skills to come up with ideas to help solve those needs.

Now it's time for them to present their ideas for your consideration. After they present they will ask you the following questions they learned to get your feedback:

1. Did you understand our idea? Is there anything you didn't understand? If so, how can we make our idea clearer?

2. What are the things you like the most about our idea?

3. If this was your idea, how would you change it?

4. Do you think we can make this idea happen? Why or why not? If why not, what can we do to make it happen?

Go, Go, Show, Show! *(40 minites)*

Goal: To present (pitch) your ideas to an audience of parents, teachers, and members of your community.

Skills: Curiosity, Connection, Communication, Storytelling, Teamwork

Needs: Team Storytelling Outlines, Storyboards, Prototypes, Billboards, and Slogans, Idea ScoreCard Poster, Feedback Questions Poster, marker or writing tools.

[Give kids time to gather their pitch materials: idea prototype, completed Storytelling Outline, Storyboard, Billboard, Slogan.]

GUIDE:

Here's how the Guppy Tank works! Each team will get **3 minutes to pitch** its idea and **5 minutes to get feedback.**

129

Follow your storytelling outline and act out your pitch. Show your prototype and use your billboard and slogan so everyone remembers your idea. (Most of all, be energetic and DON'T JUST READ THE WORDS!)

Remember, at the Guppy Tank, people want to hear great ideas. Your pitch can convince them that your idea is great! And don't forget to cheer for each other!

When the coaches are answering your questions please have your team members taking notes so you can apply their suggestions to your ideas.

[One by one, ask teams to present their pitches. After each pitch, be sure that other team members cheer for the presenting team. Then, give each team time to ask two Feedback Questions from the Feedback Questions Poster - and get feedback from the GuppyTank coaches. Limit each presentation to 3 minutes, and each feedback session to 5 minutes. Be sure teams take notes about the feedback they get.]

Brain Break! (Hula) *(5 minutes)*

Goal: Give kids a chance to get active and take a break from pitch activities while the Coaches compute their scores.

Skills: Be active, move

Needs: Hulas, Music CDs and music player or streamed music

[Guide jumps up, starts the hula brain break.]

What's the Score? *(10 minutes)*

Goal: To review the standards that Guppy Tank viewers will use to score each team's idea and pitch.

Skills: Connection, Communication, Listening

Needs: Ideas ScoreCard

GUIDE

Now that our WAGi teams have made their pitches, the Guppy Tank judges will spend some time talking together about each Team's idea. Here's how the judges will be scoring your ideas.

[Take out the Ideas ScoreCard and discuss the 6 guidelines that the judges will use when reviewing each team's pitch and idea.]

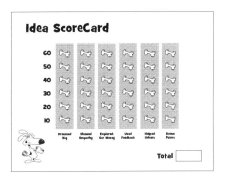

How Did You Do? Wrap Up! *(10 minutes)*

Goals: Kids share thoughts about what they've learned in the day's mission

Skills: Listening, Curiosity, Sharing, Connection, Summarizing

Needs: Storytelling Outline and Billboard Posters, Idea ScoreCard

[Sit in a circle or close together with the Storytelling Outline and Billboard Poster on display. Ask kids what they learned from getting feedback.]

GUIDE:

I'm so proud of all of you! You were amazing today! How do you feel about your Guppy Tank pitch? Were you nervous? Excited? What was the best part? Is there anything you might change next time?

How do you feel about the feedback you got? What did you learn? Will any comments help you improve your idea? Which ones?

Log In! *(5 minutes)*

Goals: Kids reflect further, and write or draw pictures in their personal logs to save their feelings, thoughts, and ideas about the GuppyTank Mission.

Skills: Reflection, Communicating ideas and feelings

Needs: Log Books

[After LogBooks have been handed out to team members.]

131

Add some thoughts or pictures to your log book to tell or show what you learned and how your Guppy Tank experience made you feel.

[After kids have finished writing in their LogBooks, collect the books.]

WAGi High Five! *(1 minute)*

Let's celebrate our day with a big WAGi High Five.

[End with a reminder about the next WAGiLab meeting!]

Idea ScoreCard

	Dreamed Big	Showed Empathy	Explored: Got Messy	Used Feedback	Helped Others	Bonus Points
60						
50						
40						
30						
20						
10						

Total

Great ideas are only great when we make them happen. Let's look at the steps we need to take to make our ideas real, and take a big step forward by writing to mentors.

We're on our way!

WAGiLabs Mission 13:

Make It Happen! *(90 minutes)*

Welcome: WAGi Cheer! *(2 minutes)*

Goals: Kids reconnect and build sense of team by chanting the WAGi Cheer

Skills: Connection, Teamwork

Needs: WAGi Cheer Poster

[As kids arrive, gather in a circle for the WAGi Cheer. Hold up the WAGi Cheer poster.

GUIDE:

It's lab day, WAGi Mates. It's time for the WAGi Cheer!

Wonder *(Arms out, palms up)*

Yes, AND *(Hi-five)*

Get Messy *(Both arms circle up & out in front of body)*

I Can *(Fist pump)*

WAGi!!!!!!

Flashback *(5 minutes)*

Goal: Reconnect kids with ideas and accomplishments from last lab experience

Skills: Curiosity, Connection, Listening

Needs: Storyboard Poster, Brainstorm Poster

GUIDE:

Last time, we pitched our ideas at the GuppyTank. What a big day!

How did you feel after you finished your pitch? How did the Guppy Tank judges respond to your ideas?

[Give kids a chance to reflect on their Guppy Tank experiences.]

If you need to make more changes to your prototype, you'll get a chance to do it later. Today, we're going to begin to talk about how to get the help we need to turn our ideas into real products, projects, and services!

Gurus and You *(20 minutes)*

Goal: To learn about different types of mentors and the guidance they offer

Skills: Curiosity, Connection, Asking Questions, Brainstorming

Needs: Mentor Poster, writing paper or board, marker or writing tool

[As a group, discuss the roles mentors play.]

Alright! Before we think about people who can help you turn your idea into a real solution, let's talk about people who have already helped you in other parts of your life.

Do any of you play an instrument or sport?

[For those who respond yes, ask if someone helped them learn to play. Suggest that teachers or coaches, in sports, music, and all areas are mentors – people who help us stretch our knowledge, improve our skills, and move towards our goals. Mentors are often experts in a specific area. Start a list of types of mentors.

Brainstorm about other mentors who have helped kids, such as teachers, parents, an older brother or sister, a neighbor, someone in the community, etc. Add these mentors to your list. Ask, too, if kids been mentors for others. Talk about the areas in which they have gotten or given advice, e.g., sports, music, cooking, art, computers, gymnastics, electronics, pet care, etc.]

Anytime you start something new, you have a lot to learn. This is especially true when you are working on a new idea or starting a new business or service.

[Ask if the WAGi kids have already had mentors who helped with their ideas, prototypes, or plans. How did these mentors help? What did kids learn? Did they avoid mistakes? Discuss details. Add the mentors to your growing list.]

GUIDE:

Working with the right mentors can help you save time, improve your idea, and avoid making mistakes.

[Have kids sit with the members of their idea team. As a full group, choose from the existing mentor list and brainstorm other mentors who might help each team with their product or service (or if teams prefer, let kids brainstorm on their own).

Possibilities include: relative/friend, community member (teacher, business person, mechanic, doctor, expert), someone at a company with a similar product/service, a content or design expert who might know how to make their product/create their service, etc. Be sure each team makes a list of at least 3 possible mentors.

End the activity by asking each team to choose one mentor from their list to write to. If kids don't have specific names of possible mentors, reassure them that together you will do research to fill in actual names.]

Make It Write! *(20 minutes)*

Goal: *To learn the purpose of an inquiry letter, to write a letter to potential mentors*

Skills: *Connection, Communication, Writing Skills*

Needs: *Letter to Mentor Poster, Mentor List, writing paper, marker or writing tools or computer with word processing program*

[Have kids gather in a circle and hold up the Write to a Mentor Poster. Hand out paper and writing tools.]

GUIDE:

Now that you've chosen a mentor to write to, what should you write? What would you want to tell a mentor about your idea?

[Brainstorm about what a letter to a mentor might say. Be sure kids understand the importance of explaining the idea and how people will use it, and also including a drawing or photo of the prototype. Respond to ideas with "Yes, AND."]

GUIDE:

Okay, let's write our mentor letters. Be sure to explain what your idea is and how people will use it. Come up with your own letter, or use this letter as a guide.

137

[Display the Letter to Mentor Poster.]

[Note: Be sure kids realize that the blue text gives instructions to help fill in the blanks in the message – the actual letter shouldn't have any blanks! If kids don't have a specific mentor name, have them write letters based on the type of mentor they are seeking. Specific names can be filled in later. Remind kids to decide which materials they want to include to give more information about their idea.]

[Hand out paper and writing tools or let teams take turns typing their letters on the computer. Suggest that kids read each message aloud and proofread it to be sure it flows and has no mistakes. Walk around the room and offer help if necessary. Give a 5-minute warning before the end of the activity. If kids need more time to finish their letters or gather copies of materials, feel free to extend the activity after the Brain Break.]

Brain Break! (Off-Balance) *(5 minutes)*

Goal: Give kids a chance to get active and take a break from discussion activities.

Skills: Physical coordination, balance

[Jump up.]

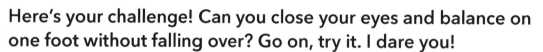

GUIDE:

Woohoo! You've been working hard on those mentor letters. It's time to get up and get physical!

Here's your challenge! Can you close your eyes and balance on one foot without falling over? Go on, try it. I dare you!

[Let kids try balancing. Many might have trouble. It's okay for them to keep their eyes open. If some kids are successful, challenge them to try balancing on the other foot. Suggest that practicing with eyes open then with eyes closed can improve your balance greatly!]

Step by Step! *(30 minutes)*

Goal: To help teams get organized and think about resources and actions needed to launch a product or service

Skills: Curiosity, Connection, Organization & Planning

Needs: 1 copy of the Timeline for each Wagi Mate, Steps Towards Making Our Idea

Real Poster, Idea Timeline Poster, Germs Prototype Poster, marker or writing tool

Prep: Print out 1 copy of the Steps Poster and one copy of the Idea Timeline for each team member

PART 1: Choosing Steps

[Have the WAGi kids gather in a circle.]

GUIDE:

Writing a letter to a mentor is a giant step toward making your ideas real. Let's think about some of the other steps you can do, and make a timeline to plan when to do each step.

[Show the Stop Germs Prototype Poster. Have kids do a hand vote to choose the idea they think will make the best product or service.

Hold up the Steps to Make Your Idea Real Checklist. Explain that the first page shows steps related to the making of a product. Which ones do kids think they'd have to take to make the Stop Germs idea real?

Show the second page of the checklist, and have kids choose the steps they'd take to get the Stop Germs idea to market. Answer any questions kids have about unfamiliar words like marketing, distribution, etc.

Guide the discussion to include doing final prototype testing and revision, connecting with mentors and businesses that make similar products, creating artwork or designs, building the final products, planning and implementing the services, and raising money to pay for components and outside manufacturers, doing advertising, marketing, and sales.]

GUIDE:

Now, let's apply these steps to your ideas!

What steps will you have to do to turn your idea into a real product, project, or service?

[Have kids split into their idea teams. Hand out a copy of the "Steps to Make Your Idea Real" Checklist and an Idea Timeline to each team member. Remind kids about the 2 Checklist parts.]

Remember, the first group of steps on this checklist relate to MAKING your product or service. The next steps are about getting your product or service to the people who need it.

Many of the steps will be the same for all teams. But, if you're offering a service or doing a project, you might need to take different steps than if you're making a product.

[Ask kids to go over both parts of the checklist with their teammates, and check off the steps they will need to do to make their idea real. Have them put 3 blue dots next to the 5 most important steps, 2 blue dots next to the next 5 most important steps, and 1 blue dot next to the steps that they will do last. Walk around the room and answer any questions.]

PART 2: Making a Timeline

[Kids continue working in small teams. Hand out a copy of the Idea Timeline to each team member.]

GUIDE:

Wow! There are a lot of steps to making your ideas happen. A timeline can help you plan which steps to do first and which come later.

Let's start by adding the steps you've already done. You've all made a storyboard and worked on one or more prototypes. What other steps have you finished?

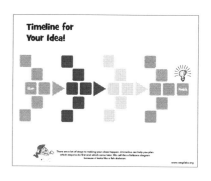

[Get other ideas from kids about steps they've completed (billboard, song, etc.). Get kids to add their completed steps at the beginning of their timeline.]

GUIDE:

Now add the steps from your checklist that you still have to do.

[Since kids have already voted on the importance of the steps, suggest that they add the most important steps to the timeline first, and keep adding steps in order

of importance. If they can't fit all of their steps on one timeline, they can leave less important steps off – or add a second timeline page.]

Wrap Up! *(5 minutes)*

Goals: Kids share thoughts about what they've learned in the day's mission

Skills: Listening, Curiosity, Sharing, Connection

Needs: Mentor Letters, Steps Towards Making Our Idea Real Checklists, Team Idea Timelines, Log Books

[Sit in a circle or close together. Have teams bring their mentor letter and Making Our Idea Real Checklist.]

GUIDE:

Today we took some big steps towards making our ideas real. Which mentor did your team write to? Why did you choose that mentor?

Were you surprised that it takes so many steps to create a new product or service? How do you feel about the steps your team has already taken towards making your idea real?

Log In! *(5 minutes)*

Goals: Kids reflect further, and write or draw pictures in their personal logs to save their feel-ings, thoughts, and ideas about the Make it Happen Mission.

Skills: Reflection, Communicating ideas and feelings

Needs: Log Books

[After LogBooks have been handed out to team members.]

GUIDE:

Add some thoughts or pictures to tell or show what you learned and how this day made you feel.

[After kids have finished writing in their LogBooks, collect the books.]

WAGi High Five! *(1 minute)*

We did a lot of detective work today, and have lots to think about! Right now, I think we need to end with a big WAGi High Five.

Letter to Mentor

_____ [FILL IN TODAY'S DATE]

Hi Mr./Ms./Dr. _____,

My name is _____, [FILL IN ONE TEAM MEMBER'S NAME] and I am __ years old. [FILL IN AGE]

I am working with my **WAGiLabs** team to come up with ideas that help make life better for people in our neighborhood and hopefully around the world. We are trying to solve the problem of:

[TELL ABOUT THE PROBLEM YOU ARE TRYING TO SOLVE. KEEP IT SIMPLE.]

My team is very interested in this problem because:

[TELL WHY YOU ARE INTERESTED IN SOLVING THE PROBLEM.]

To solve the problem, we came up with this idea:

[TELL THE NAME OF YOUR IDEA AND DESCRIBE HOW YOUR SOLUTION WORKS.]

We have attached a picture (or pictures) that shows our _____ .

[FILL IN WHATEVER YOUR PICTURE SHOWS: PROTOTYPE, DESIGN, STORYBOARD, BILLBOARD.]

We are really excited to move forward with our idea, but we need help. We think you would be a good person to talk to because

[DESCRIBE THE REASON YOU THINK THIS PERSON WOULD BE A GOOD MENTOR. FOR EXAMPLE, S/HE IS AN EXPERT, HAS A BUSINESS LIKE YOUR IDEA, HAS MADE PRODUCTS LIKE YOUR IDEA, ETC.]

We hope that you will be interested in talking to us about

[DESCRIBE THE GENERAL AREA IN WHICH THEIR EXPERTISE CAN HELP ON YOUR PROJECT, E.G., HOW WE CAN MANUFACTURE OUR PRODUCT (OR) HOW WE CAN GET OUR MESSAGE OUT TO KIDS EVERYWHERE, ETC.]

Thank you very much. We look forward to hearing from you.

Best wishes,

_____ [SIGN YOUR NAME]
_____ [LIST NAMES OF ALL OF YOUR TEAMMATES]

[FILL IN YOUR ADDRESS:]

_____ HOUSE OR BUILDING NUMBER, STREET
_____ CITY, STATE ZIP CODE
_____ PHONE NUMBER

P.S. To learn more about **WAGiLabs**, go to: www.wagilabs.org

Steps to Make our Idea Real!

Get More Feedback:

☐ Meet with mentors who have experience creating similar products/services
☐ Show idea/prototype to children or adults who will use the product/service
☐ Discuss ideas with people who will help manufacture product/service
☐ Talk to people who will help distribute your product/service

Research other Products/Services and Learn from Them:

☐ Look in Stores
☐ Search on the Internet
☐ Ask people

Test & Improve your Prototype:

☐ Make a list of materials you need to make your product
☐ Make a list of the people you will need to provide your service
☐ Schedule time to work on and revise prototype or service plan
☐ Test samples of real products and service (see/taste/use)

Create Artwork or Pictures for your Product/Service:

☐ Search for and use Clip art or images on Google
☐ Download free Animation software
☐ Download free music
☐ Find artists, photographers, musicians, actors to help you

Raise Money to pay for Manufacturing and/or Marketing:

☐ Have a Toy or Bake sale
☐ Offer services like babysitting
☐ Do a crowdfunding campaign
☐ Apply for a grant
☐ Get a loan

Manufacture Final Product/Create Final Service:

☐ Make the product or provide service yourself
☐ Find volunteers to help make your product or provide service
☐ Partner with a company to make your product or provide service
☐ Pay company to make your product or provide service

Instructions:

Check the boxes next to steps that you have to do to make your product happen.
Put 1 blue dot next to the steps that are most important, 2 blue dots next to the steps that come next, and 3 blue dots next to the steps that you would like to do if you have time.

Steps to Market and Sell our Idea!

Create a Brand:
- ☐ Come up with a name for your product or service
- ☐ Design a logo
- ☐ Write a slogan
- ☐ Write a Mission Statement that talks about your goal of helping people

Create Descriptions and Instructions for Your Product/Service:
- ☐ Write instructions telling how to use your Product/Service
- ☐ Write an explanation of how the Product/Service solves a problem
- ☐ Write descriptions to use on packaging
- ☐ Write descriptions for your website

Create Artwork or Pictures for Marketing:
- ☐ Search for images on Google
- ☐ Search for Clip Art
- ☐ Download free Animation software
- ☐ Download free music
- ☐ Find artists, photographers, musicians, actors to help you
- ☐ Shoot photos and videos of your Product/Service

Create Packaging for your Product/Service:
- ☐ Explore existing packaging
- ☐ Create new packaging with artwork, photos, and descriptions

Market your Product/Service:
- ☐ Find out how similar products/services are marketed
- ☐ Create a website
- ☐ Create a brochure
- ☐ Create a poster showing how your product/service would be sold
- ☐ Create a video
- ☐ Create a storyboard of a commercial for television
- ☐ Create an ad for a local flier, newspaper or radio

Instructions:
Check the boxes next to steps that you have to do to make your product happen.
Put 1 blue dot next to the steps that are most important, 2 blue dots next to the steps that come next, and 3 blue dots next to the steps that you would like to do if you have time.

Timeline for Your Idea!

Start

Finish

There are a lot of steps to making your ideas happen. A timeline can help you plan which steps to do first and which come later. We call this a fishbone diagram because it looks like a fish skeleton.

www.wagilabs.org

Play It Forward!

In our last session, our WAGiLab teammates reflect on their experiences, and become coaches to help other kids learn the WAGi Way.

WAGiLab Mission 14:
Play It Forward! *(90 minutes)*

Welcome: WAGi Cheer! *(5 minutes)*
Goals: Kids reconnect and build sense of team by chanting the WAGi Cheer
Skills: Connection, Teamwork
Needs: WAGi Cheer Poster

[As kids arrive, gather in a circle for the WAGi Cheer. Hold up the WAGi Cheer poster.]

GUIDE:

It's lab day, WAGi Mates. Now... it's time for the WAGi Cheer!

Wonder *(Arms out, palms up)*

Yes, AND *(Hi-five)*

Get Messy *(Both arms circle up & out in front of body)*

I Can *(Fist pump)*

WAGi!!!!!!

Flashback *(5 minutes)*
Goal: Reconnect kids with ideas and accomplishments from last lab experience
Skills: Curiosity, Connection, Listening, Compassion, Detective Skills
Needs: Make it Happen Poster, Brainstorm Poster

GUIDE:

Last time, we wrote letters to mentors and thought about the steps needed to turn our ideas into reality. Have any of you gotten a response to your letter?

[If kids have heard from mentors, discuss the responses they have received. Encourage kids to keep up the connections, and keep going with their ideas. Mention that later, you will talk more about how kids can use the WAGI website resources.]

In our very last session, you'll think about your WAGiLab experiences, and plan a talk to tell other kids about them. Sharing what you have learned in the WAGiLab is called "Playing It Forward. " It's one way to spread the word about doing good - so more people help more people!

Sharing the WAGi Ways! *(60 minutes)*

Goal: To reflect upon the WAGiLab experience, to share thoughts and coach others in the WAGi Ways.

Skills: Curiosity, Connection, Reflection, Communication, Storytelling

Needs: WAGi Ways Poster, WAGi Ways Cards, sticky notes, paper, prototypes, pitch storyboards, crayons, markers and writing tools

[Have kids count off from 1-6, and pair up by number. Hold up the WAGi Ways Poster.]

You've all grown since our first day in the WAGiLab, and so have your ideas. These six WAGi Ways have guided us as we worked together.

[Spread out the WAGi Way cards face down and let each pair choose a card. Give kids time to read the description on the back of their card.]

GUIDE:

Today, you're going to help other kids learn what it's like to be a kidpreneur by talking about the WAGi Way on the card you picked. Be sure to tell a story to help kids see the WAGiLabs experience through your eyes.

[Hand out sticky notes, paper, and writing tools. Explain that each story talk should be no more than 2-3 minutes long, including ideas from both teammates, and suggest that kids use sticky notes to plan their talk (like they planned their pitch storyboard), first writing their ideas down, and then, ordering the notes to create the best story. Encourage story teams to show storyboards, drawings, or prototypes to add visuals to their story.]

GUIDE:

Be sure to tell what you were like or how you looked at things BEFORE coming to the WAGiLab. Then tell how using the WAGi Way helped you learn or change, and why you want other kids to know about it.

we learned...
we helped...
we pitched ideas...
Before...
Join us!

[Give kids 30 minutes to plan their story talk, create new drawings, and practice with each other. Then, have pairs present to the whole group. After each presentation, encourage positive feedback and discussion of shared thoughts and experiences.]

GUIDE:

That was great! By sharing your WAGiLabs thoughts and experiences, and telling how you have grown, you can help other kids "walk in other's shoes," and see how they might grow, too.

[NOTE: If kids need more guidance for the WAGi Ways activity, here are some prompts:]

YES, and...

Before you came to WAGiLabs, were you more critical? Did you find problems with ideas instead of supporting them? Has the WAGiLab helped you be more positive and supportive? How does saying "YES, and..." encourage more ideas and make you a better team player? What can other kids learn by saying YES, and..." more often?

Dream Big!

Before you came to WAGiLabs, what ideas did you have about helping people? Were they big ideas? How have your ideas changed? Did brainstorming and working with teammates help you come up with bigger ideas? Why should other kids dream big?

Do Good!

Did you think about helping others before you came to WAGiLabs? Did WagiLabs help you have new ideas about ways to do good? How did doing detective work in the community help you learn about people who might need help? Why do you think it's important for other kids to do good?

Walk in Others Shoes!

Before you came to WAGiLabs, did you think about what other people's lives were like? What did you learn at WAGiLabs? How did walking in other shoes help you understand more about people's problems and needs? Did this change how you look at the world? Why is it important for kids to learn to walk in other people's shoes?

Get Messy!

Before you came to WAGiLabs, did you "get messy?" Did you explore lots of ideas? Did you build models and get feedback to improve your ideas? How did getting messy with your ideas at WAGiLabs change how you think? What did you learn? Why is it important for other kids to "get messy?"

Keep Going!

Before you came to WAGiLabs, did you always follow through with your ideas? How did working on a team make it easier to follow through? What did you learn about how getting feedback and revising your ideas can make them better? Why is it important to keep going? How can keeping going help other kids, too?

Brain Break! *(5 minutes)*

Goal: Give kids a chance to get active and take a break from discussion activities.

Skills: Be active, move

Needs: Music CDs and music player or streamed music from Playlist on our website

[Get kids up on their feet. Hold up the WAGi Ways poster.]

GUIDE:

You finished your stories, now let's celebrate the WAGi Ways by making up our own WAGi Ways dance moves. I'll call out a WAGi Way, and you do your dance moves to match it. When I call Switch, we'll change moves. Here we go!

[Turn on the Music. Start by calling out one WAGi Way. For the first Way (and all others, if you want), make up your own moves and dance with the kids. After 15-20 seconds, shout SWITCH!

Then give another WAGi Way. Keep going until kids have tried moves for all 6 Ways: Yes, AND…, Dream Big, Do Good, Walk in Other People's Shoes, Get Messy, and Keep Going!]

Keep Going and Going… *(20 minutes)*

Goal: Introduce the concept of persistence and resilience, encourage kids to keep going with their ideas after WAGiLabs

Skills: Curiosity, Connection, Persistence

Needs: Kids' Steps Checklists, Steps to Make Our Idea Real Poster, Grit video, marker or writing tool

GUIDE:

We've finished 14 missions together. It's hard to believe that we've come so far! Think about your WAGiLab experiences. Was it always easy to try new things? Were there times when you or your team had trouble doing something? Did you give up, or did you stick with it until you made it happen?

[Encourage kids to talk about issues they had coming up with ideas, getting and responding to negative feedback, making and changing their prototypes, creating storyboards or other presentations, working as a team, etc. Help kids focus on:

1. *What they accomplished*
2. *Specific challenges faced along the way*
3. *How they overcame the challenges*
4. *How they felt after succeeding]*

GUIDE:

Congratulations… I'd say that you have both "persistence" and "resilience." Persistence means you keep trying to reach your goal even when you face obstacles. Resilience means you bounce back and try different solutions when your first try doesn't work.

If you met some new kids who were coming to WAGiLabs, what advice would you give other kids to help them keep going when they face problems?

[Encourage kids to suggest personal tips to help other kids keep going. Support all suggestions, and congratulate the kids for having learned so much about working towards a goal. If you have access to the internet, have kids watch this simple, fun "Grit" video clip on YouTube. [https://www.youtube.com/watch?v=uwsZZ2rprqc]

GUIDE:

When you put persistence and resilience together, you get "Grit."

Persistence + Resilience = Grit

And for sure, you're going to need more grit to keep working on your idea before it becomes real. Let's brainstorm how having "Grit" will help us make our ideas happen.

[Have kids take out their Steps To Make Our Idea Real Checklist. Together, choose the steps that especially might require persistence. Make a list of these tasks and talk about how having Grit will help kids as they face each one. Suggest possible strategies to help kids keep going – and add these next to the appropriate tasks.]

153

Wrap Up! *(5 minutes)*

Goals: Kids share thoughts about what they've explored and learned in the day's mission, kids get a sense of closure for the current WAGiLabs sessions

Skills: Listening, Curiosity, Sharing, Connection

Needs: WAGiLab Website Poster, Kids' Steps Checklists, Steps to Make Our Idea Real Poster, Prototypes, Other kid-generated materials, Log Books

Prep: Print out a WAGiLab Graduation Certificate for each kid

[Sit in a circle or close together with the Steps to Make Our Idea Real Checklist, kids' prototypes, and other materials on display.]

GUIDE:

Today we talked about Playing it Forward by helping other kids learn about the WAGi Ways and helping others. We also talked about how having grit will help you move towards your goal of making your ideas happen.

Since this is our last WAGiLab, I also want to tell you about the WAGiLabs website, and how it can help you, too.

[Talk about some of the resources on the WAGiLabs website (www.wagilabs.org) that kids can use as they continue working on their ideas.]

GUIDE:

And now, I have something for each one of you – it's the official WAGiLabs Graduation Certificate of KidpreneurShip! Congratulations, WAGi Mates, you're on your way to changing the world!

[Display the WAGi Certificate and hand them out to one kid at a time and encourage applause for each kid along with taking photographs.]

Log In! *(5 minutes)*

Goals: Kids reflect further, and write or draw pictures in their personal logs to save their feelings, thoughts, and ideas about the Play it Forward Mission and the entire WAGiLabs experience.

Skills: Reflection, Communicating ideas and feelings

Needs: Log Books

[After LogBooks have been handed out to team members.]

GUIDE:

Add some thoughts or pictures to tell or show what you learned and how this day and your whole WAGiLabs experience made you feel.

[After kids have finished writing in their LogBooks, let kids keep their books so they can take them home.]

WAGi Celebration! *(5 minutes)*

Goals: Kids reconnect and build sense of team by chanting the WAGi Cheer

Skills: Connection, Teamwork

Needs: WAGi Cheer Poster

GUIDE:

Remember the first day we came together? Most of you barely knew each other. Now, you're all part of the WAGiLabs team – we've even walked in each other's shoes! Thank you for coming to WAGiLabs and sharing your ideas. Thank you for saying Yes, AND... to other kids' ideas.

Together, we discovered our passions, uncovered social needs, defined the challenge, came up with ideas, and are on our way to making them happen.

Take a minute to thank your teammates for working with you and giving so much of themselves.

[Display the WAGi Cheer poster. Chant the Cheer as you act out each step – and follow up with WAGi High Fives.]

GUIDE:

I can't think of a better way to end the day than with a big WAGi Cheer.

Wonder *(Arms out, palms up)*

Yes AND *(Hi-five)*

Get Messy *(Both arms circle up & out in front of body)*

I Can *(Fist pump)*

WAGi!!!!!!

Dream Big!

Do Good!

Dream Big!

To live life to the fullest, dream big. At WAGiLabs, we try to think of ideas that are innovative and can help many people. Dreaming big helps us do things that can change the world. What did you learn at WAGiLabs to help you dream big?

Do Good!

At WAGiLabs, doing good means coming up with ideas to help people and make the world a better place. We focus on giving rather than receiving, and acting on our ideas instead of just thinking about them. What did you learn at WAGiLabs to help you do good?

Walk in Others' Shoes!

Get Messy!

Walk in Others Shoes!

At WAGiLabs, other people inspire us to come up with ideas. When we put ourselves in other people's shoes, we see what they see or feel what they feel. Understanding others in this way is called having "empathy." What did you learn at WAGiLabs to help you walk in others' shoes?

Get Messy!

At WAGiLabs, getting messy means experimenting with ideas, models, and prototypes to come up with the best solution for a problem. Getting messy also includes getting feedback about our ideas and prototypes so we can improve them. What did you learn at WAGiLabs to help you build a prototype and get messy?

Take a Leap!

Take a Leap!

WAGiLabs is all about being positive. "YES, and..." means "I accept your idea... AND I'm ready for more!" Being open to ideas helps us learn from each other and come up with new and better ideas together. How did saying "YES, and..." help you work on ideas at WAGiLabs?

Keep Going!

Keep Going!

In the WAGiLabs, we talked about how many steps it takes to make our ideas happen. Remembering to keep going means 'not giving up' even if an idea or prototype doesn't work at first, or if you have to make changes or work hard to make your idea happen. What did you learn at WAGiLabs to help you keep going?

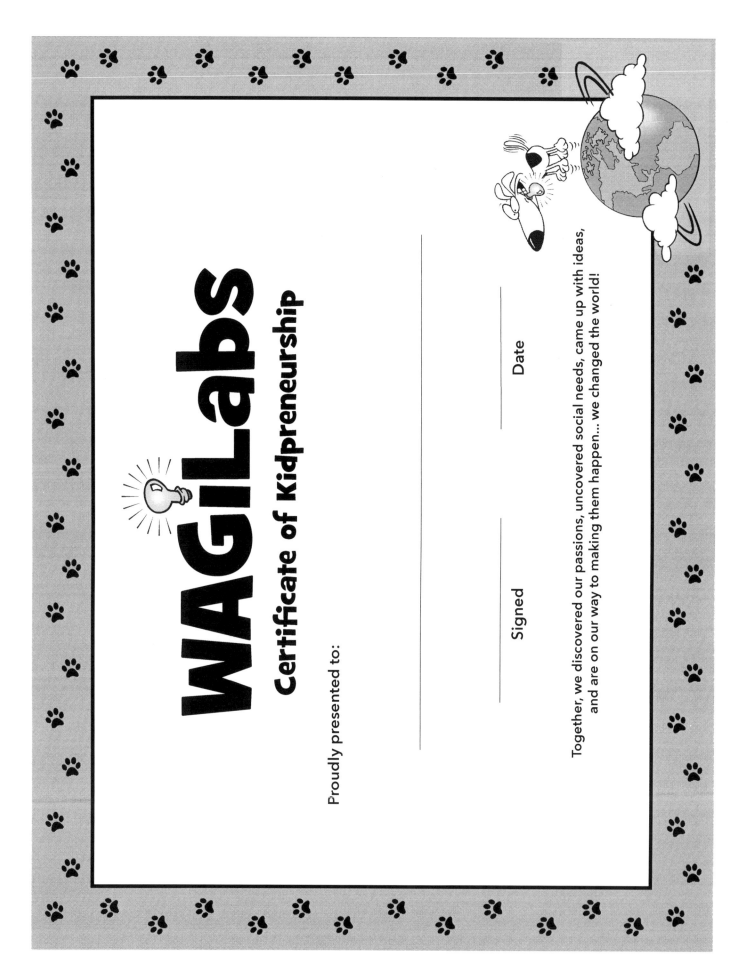

WAGiLabs

Certificate of Kidpreneurship

Proudly presented to:

_____
Signed

_____
Date

Together, we discovered our passions, uncovered social needs, came up with ideas, and are on our way to making them happen.... we changed the world!

Made in the USA
Middletown, DE
16 April 2017